Mom—and Other Great Women I've Known

Mom—and Other Great Women I've Known

Richard M. Siddoway

BOOKCRAFT
Salt Lake City, Utah

Library of Congress Catalog Card Number: 94-70344
ISBN 0-88494-923-0

First Printing, 1994

Printed in the United States of America

To all the mothers and "nursing mothers" in my life, but especially to my mother and to Geri and Janice, the mothers of my children.

Contents

1

Mother's Guilt Day

I had been called as a bishop in The Church of Jesus Christ of Latter-day Saints the last Sunday in March. Now, six weeks later, I was still getting my feet wet. Our Sunday block of meetings was over, and I sat in my office waiting for one of our youth to arrive for an interview. Sister Porter appeared in the doorway. "Bishop," she said, "do you have a moment?"

"Of course, Sister Porter, come in." I rose from my chair. She entered the office with her customary slow gait. I shook her hand. "Please, have a seat."

She shook her head. "I'll just take a minute. I wanted you to know I won't be here next Sunday to teach my class. I've asked Sister Jorgenson to cover for me." She turned to go.

"Are you taking a little vacation?" I smiled.

Sister Porter stopped at the doorway, turned, and looked back. "Oh, no, Bishop, nothing like that. It's Mother's Day."

I wrinkled my brow. "I don't understand."

"I'm not a mother," she said.

"I still don't understand. Please, sit down."

She turned slowly, closed the door behind her, and lowered herself into the chair across from my desk. "Bishop, you know I've never married. I have no children." She looked down at the carpet in front of the desk. "Every Mother's Day it's pretty painful to sit in my seat during sacrament meeting and hear about the great mothers in our ward and know I'll never be a mother. I've just chosen not to come to church on"— she paused and shrugged her shoulders—"that Sunday."

"You're not alone in these feelings, are you?" I asked.

"Probably not." A fleeting smile played on her lips. "Thanks for listening."

At that moment there was a knock on the door. My appointment had arrived. Sister Porter lifted herself from the chair and shook my hand. I walked her to the door and opened it. "Thank you for sharing your feelings with me." She nodded her head as she left, and one of the young men in our ward nervously entered for his interview.

Throughout the afternoon as I had moments between interviews I kept thinking about Sister Porter. I couldn't help wondering how many others felt the same way she did. I mentally noted the adult sisters in our ward who had never married or had never had any children. The number was fairly large.

That evening as my family followed tradition and gathered with my brothers and sisters and their children at my mother's home, I mentioned that a sister in my ward was uncomfortable with Mother's Day. Immediately my mother exclaimed, "Well, you know how your Aunt Ruth felt about it."

Aunt Ruth had married three times but had never been blessed with children. She had taken various nieces and nephews with her on vacations. My sister and I even spent an entire summer with her in Colorado Springs when she lived there. She helped several of us with college expenses and was more than generous with birthday and wedding gifts. But I did remember what she said about Mother's Day: "I'll celebrate it when they call it Aunt's Day." My Aunt Ruth always had a smile and a joke on her lips. When she talked about Mother's Day, or Aunt's Day, it was one of the few times I remember seeing her looking wistful and sad.

One of my sisters interrupted my thoughts. Shortly after her marriage she and her husband had discovered they were unable to have children. They had filed adoption papers but were still waiting. "I hate it! Maybe I'll feel differently after we . . ." Her voice trailed off. "If we ever get a baby," she concluded.

"Sorry I touched such a sore spot," I said. The conversation turned to the less volatile subjects of politics, gun control, and the death penalty.

The next day I made my way to the faculty room during my consultation period. I spread out some papers I intended to correct and began to read one of them. Three of the other faculty members crashed into the room. After retrieving cans of soda pop from the machine in the corner, they assembled themselves around one of the other tables in the room. Their conversation focused on school matters, and I tried to keep my mind on the papers I was reading, until Mrs. Carter asked loudly, "Is this Sunday Mother's Day?" The other two women nodded their heads.

"Afraid so," said Miss Halman.

"Guess I'll have to stock up on food when I go

3

shopping this week," said Mrs. Polaski. "My kids will come and give me a fifty-cent card, then eat me out of house and home."

I mentally reviewed what I knew about these three women. Mrs. Carter had married while she was in college and divorced within the year. I had never heard her speak about this experience except to indicate it was one of the "follies of youth." No children had come from this brief marriage, and she had never wed again. She had been the senior class advisor for as many years as I could remember and influenced the lives of literally thousands of students. Parents rejoiced when they found that their children were going to be taught by this kind, considerate woman.

Miss Halman was a fairly recent addition to our teaching staff. Large and somewhat awkward in appearance, she loved teaching and she loved the kids. She was an open, honest woman who gave enormous amounts of time and energy to teaching. She accepted extracurricular assignments that other faculty members refused. I remembered watching her help with dance decorations for the harvest ball and admiring her creativity. She also quietly arranged for dates for several girls who had not been asked to the dance.

Mrs. Polaski, on the other hand, had been at the school since the day it opened. She was senior member of the teaching staff and proud of it. Every day she arrived without one strand of her carrot red hair out of place. She frequently exploded with a mirthless, raucous laugh. She planned to retire at the end of this school year and was looking forward to it nearly as eagerly as her students. I learned, however, that beneath her brash exterior was an insecure, sensitive woman. She was the mother of four children. Her eldest boy was serving a term in the state penitentiary for armed robbery. She often complained that her three daughters and their families rarely visited her and that when they did it was only because they needed something from her.

"Excuse me," I interjected. "Do I detect a lack of enthusiasm about Mother's Day?"

The three women turned as one.

Mrs. Polaski brayed a laugh. "Hate it. All it means is that my kids come home and I have to fix dinner for them and all my grandbrats. They run all over the place screaming at the top of their lungs. They mess up the whole house. My husband just smiles through the whole ordeal, but I'm sure glad when they go home." She turned to the other two women for confirmation.

"At least you *have* kids to come home," said Mrs. Carter. "That's what makes me dislike Mother's Day so. You go to church and it's all geared to a typical American family—you know, Mom, Dad, one point four children." She laughed. "I've taught some of those point fours." Her face turned serious. "It's really tough when you don't fit the mold." She rose from her chair to leave, followed by Miss Halman. "It's a great idea for regular families with regular mothers, but it just doesn't fit some of us." The two of them left the faculty room.

Mrs. Polaski watched them go, then turned to me. "Do you know what the real problem is?" I shook my head. "The real problem is that when you go to church on Mother's Day the program makes you—well, at least *me*—feel guilty. Someone always gives praise to the 'perfect mother,' and I just don't fit the picture. I mean, Jason's in prison, and my three girls aren't the greatest examples in the world. I hear all those stories about these perfect women and I just feel guilty. And, of course, we always finish up with a talk about this pioneer ancestor who crawled on her hands and knees across the plains pulling a covered wagon with her twenty-six children in it. She always had time to bake twelve loaves of bread a day, read the scriptures four hours every night before retiring, milk her herd of cows, plow the field beside her husband, hand wash three hundred pieces of clothing a day, and then iron those clothes with an iron she heated on her wood-burning stove. In her spare time she cooked meals for the three dozen starving neighbors who just lost their mother to an epidemic of cholera." She smiled. "I guess I'm laying it on a little thick, but I just go home depressed at how poor a mother I've been." She downed her can of soda pop and waved good-bye as she sailed out the door.

I went back to correcting papers, when a few minutes later Miss Halman came back into the faculty room. "We were a little hard on you," she said softly. "I know you're not responsible for Mother's Day, but it's really hard on us single gals. You know that at the end of the Mother's Day program at church they always have all the mothers stand and they hand out some little gift—a plant or flower or something. I never stand, but always one of the children who are helping distribute the flowers sees me and hands one to me. I never feel that I've really earned it. I'm not a mother, and I probably never will be. I guess I feel guilty . . . and cheated somehow." She turned slowly and walked out of the room.

I thought about the Mother's Day program planned for our ward on Sunday. Indeed we were handing out flowers to the mothers, and one of the speakers was talking about his pioneer great-grand-mother who had faced all kinds of adversity. I wondered how many women we were going to offend and depress with our program.

That evening after dinner I began working on the talk I was going to give on Sunday. I turned to my wife and asked, "Honey, what would you like for Mother's Day?"

"Oh, nothing," she replied as she washed the dishes.

"Oh, come on, what would you like me to get you?"

She wiped her hands on a towel and said, "Do you really want to know, or are you just making polite talk?"

"I think I really want to know," I ventured somewhat apprehensively.

"I'd really like you to spend some time with me every day and just listen to me. You're so busy with teaching and being bishop that you really don't seem to have time to just talk with me and listen to me anymore. I know you think a box of candy or a bunch of flowers will show you love me, but just spending time with me every day is much more important. Sometimes I think husbands invented Mother's Day to try to make up for the rest of the year. They think that a five-dollar gift can make up for a whole year of inconsideration. Well, it can't. Don't spend money on me, spend time with me."

Great message. I told myself to always find time to spend with this good woman and mother of my children. I wish I could say I've always done it, but I've failed often.

As I finished writing my remarks for Sunday, I decided to give Sister Porter a call. She answered on the second ring. "Sister Porter, this is the bishop." It still seemed strange to say that. "Please come to church

Sunday. I've prepared some remarks with you in mind." She indicated that she'd think about it.

Sunday morning came and with it my first chance as bishop of our ward to talk on Mother's Day. The obligatory talks about perfect women and pioneer ancestors were given, the Primary children sang their songs with unbridled enthusiasm if lack of harmony, and then it was my turn to speak.

"My dear brothers and sisters, I am happy to be here with you today. It is a day when we honor women for their great contributions to our lives. These women are not perfect. There is only one person who was perfect, the one who, as He hung in agony upon the cross, commended the care and keeping of His mother to one of His Apostles. No, sisters, you are not perfect, but you are so much better than we men, that we choose this day to honor you. Even in your imperfections you are better than we. No one of you has been a perfect mother. None of you has perfect children. None of you has a perfect husband. I have been encouraged that in the scriptures we are told that those who will reach the celestial kingdom are 'just men'—and, I am sure, women—'made perfect through Jesus the mediator.'

"None of you mothers has spent enough time with your children. They are unfillable sponges of time. No matter how much time you spend, they demand more. It does not matter that you have attended every Little League game, every piano recital, every back-to-school night and Christmas pageant, you still have not spent enough time—no one has and no one can.

"You have not spent enough time with your husbands. We are much like children and demand more than you can give. We want you to accept us as we are, to give us affection and attention, and to demand

8

little in return. We are unfair to you, and you still support and love us.

"Those of you who have aged parents have not spent enough time with them. In many respects they have returned to a second childhood and, like children, can absorb more time than any person has available.

"This day we honor not only mothers but also those women who, as the prophets have said, are 'nursing mothers.' Born within you is a compassion that we men will never have. During this past week I have learned that Mother's Day is often painful. We have members of our ward who are not here today because they do not feel they fit the picture of 'mother.' Yet they have mothered our children. They have taught them, chastened them, and loved them. We honor them as women and 'nursing mothers.'

"To my dear wife, who often knows me better than I know myself and who accepts me with all my faults and failings, I express my love and devotion. And please join with me, all of you, as we honor our mothers, who developed the foundations upon which we built our lives."

I spoke for a few more minutes and then sat down. After the meeting a number of women thanked me for saying what I had said. One said she had been offended. I told her I was sorry and that I loved her anyway. As I left the chapel and started toward my office, Sister Porter called to me. She was sitting in the foyer. "Thank you," was all she said.

The following chapters tell stories of women I have known. Perfect? None of them. But each has been an influence in my life. Names have been changed and events altered in order to preserve the anonymity of those involved. In some cases the person described represents a compilation of individuals. The attempt has not been to deceive but to entertain with these stories of Mom and other great women.

2

Murder, Mayhem, and Motherhood

At this writing, my mother is in her eightieth year. She looks at least twenty years younger and seems to be slightly bothered that her auburn hair is starting to show a little gray at her temples. Since my father's death ten years ago, my brothers and sisters and I, their eight children, often participate in a weekly Sunday evening trek to the family home to make sure all is well with my mother. The oldest of the forty-odd grandchildren have married, and great-grandchildren are becoming a reality. Many of the younger grandchildren accompany their parents. Amid the cacophony of sound as multiple conversations are carried on in her living room, my mother dispenses ice cream and cake. There is a warm, loving feeling in this home in which we grew up. No passerby, viewing this gathering of the clan, would know what I know—my mother is not perfect. My mother makes mistakes. My mother tried to . . . well, rub me out.

I first discovered that my mother was trying to do me in when I was four years old. It was a hot summer day at our family home in Salt Lake. My little sister and I were in the backyard with my mother, who was watering the lawn by hand. The nozzle on the hose could be adjusted from a fine mist to a single jet of water. My mother misted the lawn while I played on the swing set. My little sister was seven months old and beginning to take her first steps. My mother put her in a playpen to keep her out of the water. As I swung back and forth I could see my sister standing in the playpen, holding herself upright and making wobbly exploratory attempts to stand on her feet without help.

Sweat ran pleasantly down my back as I pumped myself higher and higher in the swing. Suddenly my mother turned into a killer. Without warning she turned the nozzle of the hose until it sprayed a single stream of water and aimed it at me in the swing. The water was so cold that I felt icicles bite into my skin. I jumped from the swing and ran for the house. My mother's accuracy was amazing. The stream of water drenched me. My mother giggled. As I reached the sidewalk that ran along the back of the house my feet slipped out from under me. I skidded and slid on the water-covered sidewalk until I crashed into the milk bottles at the side of the back porch. The empty bottles exploded as I smashed them against the concrete steps. A jagged piece of glass sliced my left wrist. Blood squirted everywhere.

My mother quickly dropped the hose, which danced around like a crazed cobra, squirting water all over the backyard, including my sister in her playpen. My sister began to scream, I screamed, my mother screamed. The cobra hose was subdued, an aunt was summoned to watch my sister, and my mother took me to the doctor's office to have stitches placed in my wound. Oh, my mother feigned concern, but I knew she was trying to kill me. Never again would I venture into the backyard when my mother was watering the lawn. Well, at least not for about a week.

Eight years passed before my mother made her second attempt on my life. When I was twelve years old my family purchased a several-year-old Mercury four-door. This automobile was known for two distinguishing features: first, it was two-toned blue and gray; second, it vapor-locked whenever the outside temperature approached ninety degrees. Vapor locking meant that once the ignition was switched off, the car would not start again until it cooled down, usually at least a two-hour wait. My family had recently moved from Salt Lake to Bountiful, a small community ten miles to the north. One hot July day my mother drove our family, my brother and sister and me, to visit my Uncle Lowell and his family in Salt Lake City.

My uncle and his family lived on Fourth Avenue between A and B Streets, on the hill a few blocks northeast of Temple Square. If you parked on Fourth Avenue you climbed an almost endless flight of concrete steps to reach my uncle's front door. If you drove to Fifth Avenue and pulled down an alley you parked in my uncle's backyard. My Uncle Lowell's family included two cousins, Lowell Jr. and Nowell. My cousin Lowell was four years older than I; Nowell, two years older. Some years earlier we lived in homes a few blocks apart. Nowell and I often visited each other's homes and spent the night.

My mother parked our Mercury on Fourth Avenue, and we climbed the stairs to my uncle's front porch. My Aunt Virginia had been born in Maryland and considered herself to be the western branch of southern aristocracy. She offered us lemonade, and we sat and fidgeted for at least ten minutes in the enormous front room of their house, trying to sit properly on our chairs, before Nowell led me off to his bedroom to demonstrate two telephones he'd made from old cigar boxes and assorted electrical parts. One telephone was in his bedroom, the other ten feet away on the outside of the house near a basement window. A wire hung from Nowell's bedroom window, connecting the two phones. Nowell attached a dry-cell battery to the circuit, and I went to the outside phone. By yelling loudly we could hear each other on the telephones. Of course, we could hear ourselves more clearly through his open bedroom window, but we ignored that fact. The afternoon passed quickly. The temperature rose.

My mother announced it was time to leave. While she and my aunt descended the stairs, Nowell and I rolled, slipped, and slid down the terraced front lawn. My mother herded her children into the Mercury and attempted to start the car. It sputtered, coughed, and finally started after belching a cloud of blue smoke. We turned the corner and drove down B Street to Third Avenue, turned again, and started down the hill. At the bottom of the hill, Third Avenue intersected with the road leading out of Memory Grove. As we approached the intersection a man in a panelside truck pulled out in front of my mother. She slammed on the brakes to avoid hitting him, and our car's engine died. The driver of the truck honked his horn and waved his fist in our direction. My mother tried to start the Mercury. The engine ground but refused to start. My mother continued trying to start it until the battery was nearly dead. Vapor lock! At that moment my mother's quick mind raced to put in place the plan to murder me.

"Walk back up to Lowell's and see if he'll come help us get the car started," she said to me. I climbed back up the hill the three blocks to my uncle's home. Up the stairway I trudged. My uncle loaded Nowell and me into his ancient Dodge and drove to my mother's aid. My uncle was very good at making things work, but he was in over his head when it came to solving the vapor-lock problem in our car. He lifted the hood and tinkered for a few minutes before slamming it back down.

"I think if I push you, we can get the car started," he announced. We had never tried pushing our Mercury when it vapor-locked. My mother shrugged her shoulders and got back into our car. My uncle inched the big black Dodge forward until the bumper of his car was inches from the bumper of ours. He climbed out of the car and checked the bumpers. The front bumper of the Dodge was at least four inches lower than the rear bumper of the Mercury. My uncle checked out the misfit from every angle. "We've got to get some weight on the back of your Merc," he proclaimed. "Nowell, climb up on that blue beast." Obediently my cousin stood on the bumper of our car. Nowell was a big boy; the car dropped three of the four inches. My uncle inspected the situation. "Got to have more weight."

My mother looked at me, her mind churning out the plot. "Climb on. Let's see if that will help." I climbed onto the bumper beside my cousin. The car settled another inch or so.

"Get in," my uncle said to my mother. My mother slid into the front seat of the Mercury. I could look directly through the rear window at her behind the wheel. Nowell and I leaned forward on the trunk of the car. "Perfect fit," announced my uncle. "You boys hang on tight and I'll give you a push."

"Be careful!" called my mother from the front seat, feigning concern. My sister and brother knelt on the backseat of the car and looked out the window at Nowell and me. My uncle inched forward with his car until the bumpers engaged. Slowly he began pushing my mother toward North Temple. My cousin and I felt the bumpers shift ominously beneath our feet.

When Brigham Young and the pioneers entered the valley of the Great Salt Lake in 1847, he drove his cane in the ground and proclaimed, "Here we will build a temple to our God." That place where he planted his cane is now known as Temple Square. The four streets that bound this ten-acre block are Main (once called East Temple), South Temple, West Temple, and North Temple. As the name implies, North Temple runs east to west on the north side of Temple Square. We were westbound on North Temple about a block and a half east of Main Street.

As our cars approached State Street, a block east of Main, the traffic light turned red. My mother instinctively put on the brakes. My uncle's reflexes were not as quick, and we felt the bumper of his Dodge push under the bumper of the Mercury. With a screech and a scrape the two bumpers locked. We came to a halt. My uncle inspected the situation from every angle. "Get off, boys." We did.

Traffic began to pile up around our two interlocked automobiles. Horns honked. My uncle placed his hands on the front fender of his car and bounced

the cars up and down. The bumpers refused to separate. More horns honked. Finally three other men
climbed out of their automobiles and offered to help.
Two of them lifted up on our bumper while my uncle
and the third man tried to force his bumper down.
With a squeal of metal the two cars unlocked. My
uncle ordered Nowell and me back onto the bumper
of the Mercury. The light turned green, and we inched
forward down North Temple.

Periodically my mother let out on the clutch and the
two cars shuddered and stammered, but our Mercury
refused to start. We crept through the intersection at
Main Street. Nowell and I searched the trunk of our car
for a place to hold on to as my uncle pushed us faster
and faster down North Temple. We cleared the West
Temple intersection and chugged on toward Second
West. About a hundred feet before reaching the intersection my mother let out on the clutch and the Mercury belched a cloud of noxious fumes from its exhaust
pipe. The two cars bucked, the bumpers slid against
each other, my uncle put on his brakes, and the two
cars separated. Nowell wisely jumped off the bumper
of our car. I scrambled to retain my perch. As our car
chuffed and huffed the last hundred feet toward the intersection, the traffic light turned yellow. My mother
panicked. She did not want the car's engine to die
again. She sped up, jerkily, and zipped around the corner. I was launched from the back bumper of the car
onto the road. I landed on my left side and rolled and
skidded to the center of the intersection. Horns honked.
My mother pulled to the side of the road and stopped.
The car's engine kept on running.

Drivers jumped from several cars and raced to my
aid. My mother reached me just as I staggered to my
feet. Two quarter-size patches of skin were missing

from my left wrist. Blood oozed down my hand as my left arm hung limply at my side. People's concern changed to annoyance as I grabbed my left wrist with my right hand and weaved through the crowd to our car. "Crazy woman driver," shouted one of the crowd as he made his way back to his car. Traffic began to flow again.

I sat in the front seat trying not to drip blood on the seat cover. My younger sister and brother had begun to cry when they saw me fly off the bumper. They continued to howl from the backseat as we drove home to Bountiful. Although my mother concluded to the best of her medical knowledge that nothing too serious was wrong with me, she decided to take me to our family doctor to make sure.

After it was determined that I had no broken bones, our doctor cleaned my abrasions, applied salve, and bandaged my wrist. He looked me square in the face. "Are you mad at your mother?"

I shrugged. "Not really."

"She feels terrible, you know," he said.

"I guess so," I replied.

"Have you ever done anything that you wish you hadn't done?"

"Sure," I said, thinking of several dozen mistakes I wished hadn't happened.

"Your mother wishes she could go back and live this afternoon again. She'd do things differently."

"I'm not mad at her," I exclaimed as I tried to raise my left arm. It was stiff and sore but seemed to be movable. I jumped down from the examining table and joined my mother in the waiting room. She looked as if she were in worse shape than I. She took me to the Servus Drug on the way home and bought me a root beer float.

My mother has become much more subtle in her attempts on my life since that hot July afternoon. Now she just stuffs me with high-cholesterol foods when we visit her home.

3

The Home of the Brave

There was a time in my life when I thought Mrs. Pierce was the bravest woman in the world. She almost convinced me of that during the summer of 1950, when I was ten years old.

Mark Pierce lived across the street from my cousin Bill. They both lived a block east of the old state penitentiary, which added a flair of excitement when I stayed overnight with Bill. My mother was convinced we'd be killed or at least taken hostage if any prisoners escaped. Between the prison buildings and my cousin's house were the prison vegetable gardens. A cornfield hugged the barbed-wire fence at the end of Bill's road. We considered ourselves quite daring when we stood outside that fence and talked to the trustees who weeded the cornfield.

Bill and I enjoyed a special relationship, since Bill had lived with my family for nearly two years while his house was being built. Mark had replaced me as Bill's best friend when the two of them moved across the street from each other. At first I was extremely jealous, but then Mark and I became friends, too.

One morning in early June, Bill's mother offered to pay us each a quarter if we'd clean up the yard. Although Bill's family had lived in their home for a year and a half, there was still a pile of junk, left over from the construction, lying on the west side of their house. My uncle conducted a running battle with the contractor over whose responsibility it was to clean up the mess. My aunt finally ran out of patience and was willing to pay us three boys to clean it up.

At first the task looked as daunting as the Aegean stables, but before long we created a game out of moving and stacking the short pieces of lumber, lath, wire, and empty paint buckets. Near the bottom of the pile of debris was a piece of plywood about two feet square. Bill picked it up and uncovered a snake. I do not know whether our fear of snakes reached back to Eden, or whether we triggered each other's visceral response, but I do know the three of us screeched a soprano chorus in unison. The snake coiled. Bill threw the piece of plywood into the air.

I am sure none of us had heard a rattlesnake before. But as we paused in our terrified screaming, we heard the warning buzz of the snake's tail and knew exactly what it was. Our second shriek was louder than the first. Windows in the neighborhood were in danger of shattering. Paralyzed with fright, the three of us stood anchored to the spot.

Children often scream. How parents can tell the difference between screams of anger, of pain, or of terror, I do not know, but I do know they can. Mrs. Pierce was weeding the garden behind her home when Bill discovered the snake. Our first scream galvanized her into action. Before our second chorus died on the air, she rounded the corner of Bill's house at a dead run, hoe in hand. We three boys stamped our feet, our legs pumping up and down, our fingers pointing at the coiled rattlesnake. In one swift action, Mrs. Pierce brought the hoe down on the back of the rattlesnake's head, then reached down with her other hand and grabbed the snake by its tail. She drew the snake up in an arc and snapped it, just as a person cracks a whip. The snake's head popped off.

Mrs. Pierce threw the still-writhing body down on the ground and beat it with her hoe. Although the snake seemed about forty feet long when we first viewed it, as it stopped wriggling it shrank until it was less than two feet in length. She draped the dead reptile over the head of the hoe, picked up the snake's head with her gloved hand, and said stiffly, "I'll just bury this old fellow."

She walked back across the road while the three of us lied to each other.

"Boy, you two sure were scared," said Bill, scraping his toe in the dirt.

"You screamed the loudest," said Mark.

"Did not," exclaimed Bill.

"Did too."

"Did not."

Apparently Mrs. Pierce buried the snake. We refused to do any more cleanup.

At the time Bill discovered the snake, my aunt was at the grocery store. When she returned home, ten minutes after Mark's mother dispatched the rattler, Bill gloried in telling her the story. The events changed a little, with Bill becoming the hero who protected Mark and me from certain death. In my heart I knew

Mrs. Pierce was the bravest woman alive. My aunt raced across the street to the Pierces' home and learned the true story. She phoned my uncle at his law office and informed him.

Bill's creative mind often led him down paths that caused my uncle considerable grief. This event gave my uncle some ammunition. When he got home he said to Bill, "Just stood there screaming? Mrs. Pierce had to rescue you?" He chuckled. Bill was not pleased.

Two weeks later I was sleeping over at Bill's house again. "You want to earn another quarter?" Bill asked.

"I dunno. Do we have to clean up your yard?" The sound of the rattlesnake was still fresh in my mind.

"Nah," said Bill. "That dumb Mrs. Pierce needs to have some bottles unpacked and put on the shelves in her basement. She'll give us each a quarter."

"Why do you call her dumb?" I asked.

"She kept me from killing that rattlesnake. Dad just keeps rubbing it in."

"But she saved our lives," I countered. Bill just snorted and turned over in his bed. Although Bill handed out abuse quite liberally, he had difficulty absorbing it.

The next morning Bill, Mark, and I crept down the stairs into the Pierces' basement. The entire north wall was covered with newly constructed shelves. I could smell the odor of freshly cut lumber. On the west wall were forty or fifty cardboard boxes stacked three high. "Boys," Mrs. Pierce said, "those boxes are filled with bottles of fruit and vegetables I've canned over the past several years. I've written on the outside of each box what's inside. All you need to do is open the boxes and put the bottles on the shelves. Just put the peaches together, the beans together, and so forth. Do you think you can do that without breaking any bottles?" The three of us nodded our heads. "Well, just be careful. Call me if you have any questions." She clumped back up the basement stairs.

"Maybe we ought to sort the boxes first," suggested Bill. Whoever carried the boxes of bottled produce down to the basement had not taken time to stack the boxes in any specific order. Boxes of bottled peaches were scattered among the boxes containing many other items. Bill grabbed the first box. It weighed more than he anticipated and he nearly dropped it. Quickly he slid it back into place. "Let's just open them and arrange the bottles on the floor. Then we can put them on the shelves." Feverishly we opened boxes and sorted bottles of peaches, cherries, apricots, pears, beans, peas, pickles—actually dill pickles, sweet pickles, mustard pickles, and pickled tomatoes—into areas on the basement floor. There were nearly five hundred bottles.

Mrs. Pierce came down the stairs to check on our progress. "I want them on the shelves," she challenged, "not on the floor."

"Mom," Mark anguished, "we're just sorting them out before we put them on the shelves." Mrs. Pierce shrugged her shoulders and turned to go back up the stairs, when suddenly she let out a shriek. The bravest woman in the world stepped backward three quick steps, sending bottles of pickles flying. We three boys sprang into action, moving as far away from the steps as possible.

"Mark!" screamed Mrs. Pierce. "There's a spider on the stairs!" She pointed wildly at the bottom step. Mark picked up a short piece of lumber, weaved through the maze of bottles until he was beside his mother, and squished the spider with the board. It was, or had been, a small brown spider about the size of a pencil eraser. "Can't stand them," Mrs. Pierce shuddered. "They give me the willies." She carefully inspected each step as she climbed the stairs to her kitchen.

"Your mother's afraid of spiders?" chortled Bill. "She kills snakes with her bare hands, but she's afraid of spiders?"

"Yeah," said Mark, "she can't stand 'em. Don't know why." He shrugged his shoulders. A terrible, wicked smile crossed Bill's face.

Miraculously none of the bottles had been broken by Mrs. Pierce's kicks. Within the hour we completed the task of stacking bottles on shelves. The empty cartons were carried out to the garage. Not only did Mrs. Pierce pay us a quarter, but she gave us each an ice-cream cone. Bill and I waved good-bye to Mark and ambled across the street to Bill's house. We sat on his front porch, slowly licking the ice cream.

"Scared of spiders," Bill mused. "Mark's mom is scared of spiders. I'm going to pay her back!"

"Pay her back for what?" I asked.

"For all the teasing my dad's given me." Bill's convoluted thinking sometimes confused me. "Ever since she killed that snake my dad's been laughing at me. Well, we'll see who laughs now." He smirked and chuckled, and licked his ice cream.

An hour later my aunt announced she had some shopping to do. Bill and I loved to go shopping with his mother. She was a pushover when we asked for treats. To her surprise, and mine, Bill announced we didn't want to go.

As soon as my aunt left, Bill began searching in the kitchen cupboards. "I know we have some paraffin here somewhere." He moved to the drawers beside the refrigerator. "Ah, here it is." He unwrapped one of the sticks of paraffin my aunt used to seal the bottles of jelly she made each year. Bill tried to cut off a small piece of paraffin, failed, and put the whole stick in a saucepan. While the wax began melting on the stove, Bill rummaged around in an old shoe box he kept in his closet. Between a shoehorn and some ski wax Bill found half a large black crayon. He peeled off the paper and added the crayon to the melting paraffin.

A piece of waxed paper was spread on the kitchen table and onto it Bill poured a melted glob of dark gray wax. As soon as the paraffin had hardened on the outside, Bill began molding it into the shape of a large spider's body. Four strands of my aunt's black embroidery thread were stuck across the body to provide the spider's eight legs. Bill finished off his creation by painting a large red hourglass shape on the top of the spider. He picked it up, turned it over in his fingers, and chuckled with satisfaction.

I thought his creation looked about as much like a spider as Harry Truman looked like Rin Tin Tin, but Bill was satisfied. We tried to wash the rest of the paraffin out of the saucepan and found it impossible. Bill carried the pan down into the basement and threw it through the opening into the crawl space beneath his living room. "Let's go," he said. "It's time to pay Mrs. Pierce back!"

Bill led the way across the street to the Pierces' home. Mark's home was built in the shape of a shallow L. The front porch ran along the backbone of the L, and Mrs. Pierce's bedroom stuck out alongside the front porch. There was a window that looked onto the porch from the bedroom. As we climbed the steps to the front porch, I thought I saw the curtains in Mrs. Pierce's bedroom move slightly. Bill held the "spider" tightly in his hand. The still-warm paraffin squished between his fingers. He pushed his creation against the screen door and it stuck.

Bill signalled me to run back across the street. Then he flattened himself against the wall beside the front door, reached out furtively, and rang the doorbell. Almost immediately the front door flew open. Mrs. Pierce squinted out into the bright sunlight. Suddenly she threw the screen door open and stepped out onto the porch. Bill bolted for the steps just as Mrs. Pierce screamed in mock horror and swatted at the screen with a rolled-up newspaper. The "spider" flew through the air and landed on Bill's back. In a flash Mrs. Pierce grabbed Bill's arm and began swatting the "spider," and Bill's back, with the newspaper. Bill screamed and wiggled to get free.

"Hold still! There's a spider on your back!" Mrs. Pierce continued to swat Bill with the newspaper until he finally escaped and ran across the street, yelling at the top of his lungs. Mrs. Pierce went back in the house.

That summer I learned that Mrs. Pierce was not only the bravest woman in the world but also one of the smartest.

4

She Who Is Without Sin

My father and mother began looking for a bigger house when my mother was expecting their sixth child. At the time, we owned an enormous green Hudson Hornet, and all seven members of our family squeezed into it to go house hunting. My father was known as a careful shopper, and we anticipated a several-month-long search. Perhaps the noise created by five children crammed into the backseat of the Hudson accelerated my father's decision to buy a house after only two days of looking.

The day we began carrying boxes into the house, our next-door neighbors appeared and offered help. I was delighted to find that a thirteen-year-old boy, Dale, was part of the family. I was fourteen at the time. Dale and I struck up a fast friendship, and with him I scouted the neighborhood. We lived only three blocks from the Servus Drug, where for thirty-five cents we could buy a sundae big enough to satisfy even our teenaged penchant for ice cream. Sometimes we arrived close to the nine o'clock closing hour and Ted, the owner, offered us a free piece of Grandma Nell's homemade pie.

Dale, of course, had other friends, and it is to their credit that they accepted me willingly into their fold. Stick (all seventy-five pounds of him), Kelly, Roger, and Larry all became fast friends of mine. One day as Dale and I walked over to Stick's house we took a different route than usual. I was throwing a baseball in the air and trying to catch it. I threw it as high as I could and missed it. The ball bounced on the sidewalk and over a short white picket fence onto the most meticulously groomed lawn I had ever laid eyes on. I started to step over the fence, when Dale grabbed me by the arm. "Uh-oh, we're in trouble," he said. "Sister Michaelis will be out the door any minute." At that moment the front door flew open, and out burst Sister Michaelis.

She was wearing a light beige suit with a frilly blouse. Although her face was covered with a veil that was attached to the brown pillbox hat on her head, I could tell that her makeup was flawless. "You boys," she called, "don't step on the lawn. You'll mar it." We stood like statues while she pranced around the corner of the house in her high-heeled shoes. In a moment she returned with a rake in her carefully gloved hand. "Here, boy, retrieve your ball with this."

I took the rake from her, reached over the fence, and pulled the ball to me. I handed her the rake and caught a delicious whiff of floral perfume. "I'm sorry," I said. "I didn't mean to throw the ball on your lawn."

"Just be more careful in the future." She disappeared around the corner of the house. I took a closer look at the house. The paint gleamed white and spotless. The evergreens at each corner of the house had been pruned to exact cone shapes. The rose garden on the east side of the house was weed-free and edged with paving stones. There was not one thing out of place.

"That's a neat house," I exclaimed.

"Yeah," said Dale, "there isn't a weed in town that would dare grow there."

"I wonder where she's going dressed like that. My mom doesn't even dress up that much to go to church."

Dale shrugged. "She always looks that way. You'll never see her without her being dressed to the teeth. She's kind of strange that way." We went on our way to Stick's house.

Sunday that week was the first Sunday of the month. In The Church of Jesus Christ of Latter-day Saints, that means sacrament meeting will be a fast and testimony meeting. Following the blessing of babies, the confirmation of newly baptized members, and the sacrament, members of the ward stand and bear their testimonies. Frequently members recount faith-promoting experiences; often they give expressions of thanks for kindnesses extended by others. Most of the people speaking just stand at their seats and speak. That Sunday, Sister Michaelis suddenly stood and strode to the front of the chapel. Dale and his family were sitting in the row behind my family. I heard Dale's father whisper, "Uh-oh, here she goes."

I glanced back. Dale's face was white with fear. "We're gonna get it for throwing the ball on her lawn," he whispered.

Sister Michaelis stood at the pulpit and grasped both sides with her glove-clad hands. She was wearing a broad-brimmed white straw hat and a pale gray suit. She cleared her throat. "Ahem. Brothers and sisters." She paused for effect. "The Lord said, 'My house is a house of order.' I believe that means when we see something out of place, we need to take care of it."

"Here she goes," whispered Dale's father.

"Just this last evening I couldn't help but notice that Bishop Grover's daughter was out with a young man until nearly midnight. Bishop, do you think that is proper behavior?" She glanced back over her shoulder.

Bishop Grover smiled a weak smile and shook his head.

Sister Michaelis must have established quite a grapevine for gathering information, because she continued for nearly ten minutes recounting every indiscretion in the ward. Apparently baseballs ranked fairly low on her scale of sin, since I was not brought to task until the very end of her "testimony." "There is a new family in our ward who need to instruct their children in proper behavior," she pontificated. "Their teenaged son threw his baseball onto my lawn this past week. Thankfully we were able to retrieve it without damage. It could have landed just as easily in my roses as on my lawn. I am sure we all know what would happen to society if we displayed wanton disregard for other people's property."

"She's winding down," whispered Dale's father.

"Now, brothers and sisters, I hope you realize that I have been speaking out of love and concern for the people of this ward. We have a good ward and we want to keep it that way." She concluded with a few words of actual testimony and then walked quickly back to her seat. A few minutes later the closing hymn and prayer ended the meeting.

Dale and I walked home together. "Does Sister Michaelis do that every testimony meeting?" I asked.

"I think so. At least I can't remember one where she didn't call us all to repentance. Everybody's kind of used to it. She's just kind of a perfect person. I mean, her house is perfect, she's perfect, and she can't understand why the rest of us aren't perfect."

"I think I'll just stay away from her," I said.

"That's what everybody does," replied Dale.

That afternoon Bishop Grover came to visit our family. When he discovered that I was fourteen years of age and a teacher in the Aaronic Priesthood, he indicated that Brother Feldman needed a ward teaching companion. Ward teachers went every month, two by two, to visit members of the ward, each pair being assigned two or three families. The ward teachers gave a short lesson and generally made sure the members' needs were being met. I had no idea who Brother Feldman was, but the bishop told me he'd have him get hold of me.

An hour later, Brother Feldman called. "I like to go ward teaching the first week of the month," he said. "Would Tuesday night be convenient?"

"I guess so," I said.

"Good. I'll pick you up about seven. We just have three families to visit, the Dahlbergs, the Stallingses, and Sister Michaelis."

Tuesday evening Brother Feldman pulled up in his car in front of my family's house and honked his horn. I remembered him from church. He was almost completely bald except for a coal black fringe of hair. He shook my hand as I climbed into his car. "We'll go see the Dahlbergs first," he said. "They go to bed pretty early."

I couldn't believe that anyone went to bed at seven o'clock in the evening, but when we arrived at the Dahlbergs' home, Brother Dahlberg was dressed in pajamas and a bathrobe. I couldn't remember having seen either one of them before. Brother Feldman introduced me, and we walked into their backyard and sat on some folding chairs. "Pretty hot one today, eh?" said Brother Feldman.

"Been a hot summer," said Brother Dahlberg. He appeared to be in his late sixties, heavyset and with a three- or four-day growth of whiskers. Sister Dahlberg was a little bird of a woman. She perched on the edge of her chair and rocked back and forth for the few minutes we visited. Brother Feldman and Brother Dahlberg carried on a conversation about the weather and the possibility of irrigation water lines being completed in the next couple of years. Sister Dahlberg just rocked back and forth. I smiled at her. She smiled back.

"Well," said Brother Feldman, "I hope everything is going well for you. We'll see you next month."

"Everything's fine," said Brother Dahlberg. "Thanks for coming." We shook hands and walked back around to Brother Feldman's car.

"They're good people," he said. "Haven't seen them in church for a long time, but they seem to enjoy having us visit."

"Sister Dahlberg seems kinda quiet," I ventured.

"I think she's just shy. I don't think I've heard her say three words in the five years I've been visiting them. Well, let's go over to the Stallingses'. They're quite a different family." We drove down the street two houses.

I could hear a baby crying as we climbed out of the car. We walked up the steps to the front door and rang the bell. Immediately the door was opened by a little boy about three years of age. He was standing stark naked in the doorway. "Hi, Scotty," said Brother Feldman. "Are your mom and dad home?"

Scotty turned around and screamed at the top of his lungs, "Mommy, the bald man's here!"

Sister Stallings called out, "Please come in. I'm just getting Jennifer her bottle." We walked into a beehive of activity. Scotty and his two younger twin brothers were running around the front room without a stitch of clothing. There were piles of clothing everywhere. Sister Stallings appeared from the kitchen carrying a baby in her arms. She was a plump, apple-cheeked woman of about thirty years. She stuck her hand out to Brother Feldman. "Glad to have you here, Brother Feldman. Scotty, Cal, Hal, stop running! I mean it, this minute!" The boys kept on running around. "I was just getting them ready for a bath, when Jennifer started crying for her bottle."

Brother Feldman introduced me, and Sister Stallings grasped my outstretched hand and shook it firmly. "Glad to have you visit, anytime. Cal, leave Hal alone! Scotty, sit down! I'm sorry Jerry's not home. He just ran down to get some things at the store. He'll be back any minute. Cal, I mean it, leave Hal alone!"

Brother Feldman reached over and put an arm around Cal, or was it Hal? He scooped him up into his arms and said, "Ready for a bath?" Cal/Hal squirmed and pushed against Brother Feldman's chin.

Sister Stallings reached out with her free arm and shoved the pile of clothing off the couch. "Have a seat."

Brother Feldman decided not to sit. He put Cal/Hal down and said, "We don't want to stay long. I can see you're busy. Is everyone well?"

"We're just fine, Brother Feldman. And we really appreciate your concern. Scotty, take Cal and Hal to the bathroom. I'll be there in a minute." The boys actually exited the room. Sister Stallings deftly balanced Jennifer in her left arm, tucked the bottom of the bottle under her chin, and shook hands with Brother Feldman and me as we exited.

"Always a lot of activity in that house," commented Brother Feldman as we climbed into his car. "Four children under four years of age. Sister Stallings really has her hands full. I wish Brother Stallings had gotten there in time for you to meet him. He's a really nice young man. I'll introduce you to him at church next Sunday."

We drove around the corner. "Ah," said Brother Feldman apprehensively, "Sister Michaelis can be a challenge. Let's go see how the wind is blowing tonight. Oh, stay on the sidewalk, don't walk on the lawn." We walked slowly and carefully up her front walk. Before we reached the front porch Sister Michaelis opened the door and stepped out. She was dressed in a black evening dress complete with elbow-length gloves. She had a flat black hat on her head and a rope of pearls around her neck. She extended her hand, thumb and fingers together, palm down, as if she expected Brother Feldman to kiss the back of her hand. He touched her hand with his. "Good evening, Sister Michaelis."

"Brother Feldman." She nodded her head. "And the, uh, new boy in the ward." She smiled a frozen smile in my direction. "Please do come in." She swept us into her living room with a flourish of her arm and hand.

I watched Brother Feldman scrub the bottoms of his shoes on the doormat. I did the same and stepped gingerly onto her snow white carpet. The room was decorated all in white, with accents of color placed here and there. Centered between two armchairs was a blood red vase nearly four feet high, filled with plumes of pampas grass. The crystal coffee table had a goblet filled with transparent red, blue, and clear marbles. A huge mirror covered the wall above the marble fireplace. On the mantel was a single scarlet rose in a crystal vase. Nothing was out of place.

"Brother Feldman, I am so glad you came tonight. I've been having a little, teensy problem and I wonder if you can help me." Without pausing for an answer she continued. "Those beastly Stallings children are always throwing things over the fence into my backyard. I wonder if you could talk to them for me. They seem to get so offended if I talk to them. Could you? Would you? Hmmm?"

I looked closely at Sister Michaelis and tried to determine her age. In the subdued light of her living room she could have been anywhere between her late forties and her early seventies. Her makeup was flawless, but there was just the slightest hint of a tremor in her voice. Brother Feldman agreed to talk to the Stallings family. "And how are you, Sister Michaelis?"

"Just fine, Brother Feldman, just fine." She fixed an icy gaze on me. "It's such a pleasure to have new members move into the ward." I smiled weakly back at her as I shrank into my chair. "Especially well-mannered ones." She smiled at Brother Feldman. "Well, I shan't keep you all evening." She rose, and we shook her limp hand and walked carefully from the house. As we climbed into Brother Feldman's car I thought I could hear the sound of a vacuum cleaner coming from Sister Michaelis's house.

"She's an interesting woman," Brother Feldman said, rubbing his chin. "We got off easy tonight. Sometimes it takes over an hour to get out the door. She usually has a list of people who have offended her one way or another and who she wants me to go set straight."

"Is she married?" I asked. "Does she have any children?"

"I really don't know much about her. She moved into this house about ten years ago. She lives alone. I've never seen anyone visit her. Some people say her husband died; others think he left her because he couldn't stand perfection. It pains me to tell you that I have visited her as her ward teacher for nearly six years and I don't know much at all about her. Of course she does try to control the conversation."

And everything else, I thought to myself.

"I know that on Mother's Day she always refuses the little plants they hand out to the mothers in our ward, but I always thought it was because they didn't fit her decorative scheme." Brother Feldman drove me home and suggested that we make it a regular appointment to do our ward teaching the first Tuesday of every month. We shook hands and he drove off.

Our August ward teaching visits were much the same, except that the Stallings children were dressed. In the August fast and testimony meeting Sister Michaelis spent nearly fifteen minutes confessing others' sins. During our September ward teaching visit Sister Dahlberg actually said, "Hello." In October I finally met Brother Stallings.

The first Tuesday of November, Brother Feldman picked me up at seven o'clock. It was a cold November. Snow had fallen before Halloween. The residue of fallen leaves filled the gutters. We walked up the sidewalk to the Dahlbergs' front porch. A dummy made from an old pair of coveralls stuffed with newspaper still sat in the corner of the porch. We rang the doorbell. Brother Dahlberg answered the door and invited us in. "Pretty cold one today, eh?" said Brother Feldman.

"Been a cold winter," said Brother Dahlberg. He sat down heavily in his rocking chair. Sister Dahlberg perched on the edge of the couch. She smiled at me and I smiled back. Brother Dahlberg and Brother Feldman talked about the weather and whether the Weber Basin irrigation lines were going to be in place by the next summer.

Suddenly Sister Dahlberg said, "I thought we might come to church on Christmas." Brother Dahlberg and Brother Feldman turned in unison to stare at her. I smiled.

"We'd be pleased to see you there," I said.

She went back to rocking on the edge of the couch. Brother Feldman and I shook hands with the Dahlbergs and left.

"Amazing," said Brother Feldman. "I've never heard her say that much before. I hope she follows through and they come."

"Maybe we could offer to take them," I ventured.

"We'll see," said Brother Feldman. "I don't want to push them too hard and destroy the good feelings we've built up."

Both Brother and Sister Stallings were home, as were their four children. After a five-minute visit, we left.

We walked carefully up Sister Michaelis's sidewalk. There were leaves on her grass. *That's odd,* I thought. Brother Feldman rang the bell. No one answered, although there was a light on in the front room. We rang the bell again. Again there was no answer. Brother Feldman turned to go.

"I guess she's not home. We'll have to come another time."

"Brother Feldman. I think something's wrong. Just look at the front yard. She's got leaves on her lawn.

Can you really believe Sister Michaelis would have leaves on her lawn?"

We paused for a moment, and then Brother Feldman walked back up the stairs to the front porch, stood on tiptoes, and peered through a small window in the door. "Oh no . . ." He banged on the door. "I can see Sister Michaelis lying on the floor. Quick, run around to the back door and see if it's open."

I ran around the house and tried the back door. It opened. I called to Brother Feldman, then stepped into the kitchen and fumbled for a light switch. When the lights came on I couldn't believe my eyes. I had never seen such clutter. There were dirty dishes and pots and pans stacked everywhere. Open boxes and cans of food were on the counter, the table, and the floor. Just as Brother Feldman came through the back door, I saw the empty vodka bottle in the sink.

"What in the world? I can't believe this is Sister Michaelis's house!" He pushed his way through the clutter to the door to the living room. Sister Michaelis was lying on the snow white carpet next to the couch. Brother Feldman felt for a pulse and found one. We lifted her onto the couch. Her eyes fluttered open.

"What . . . what are you doing here?" Her eyes darted to the open kitchen door. Then tears came to her eyes and she began to sob. Brother Feldman cradled her in his arms. "No one. No one has seen any other room in my house for years. No one."

"It's all right, Sister Michaelis. It's all right. You need a tissue. Do you have any?"

She looked frightened, but she waved in the direction of another door. "In there."

I walked into Sister Michaelis's bedroom. There were bigger piles of clothing than I had seen at the Stallingses' home. The bed appeared not to have been made in weeks. I found a box of tissues on the dresser and took it back into the living room.

"I haven't been feeling well," Sister Michaelis was saying. "It's an old illness I thought I was over. But I'll be fine now. Thank you so much for coming." She waved us out the front door.

We walked down the steps to Brother Feldman's car. I wondered if he had seen the vodka bottle. "My boy," he said, "do you know how to keep your mouth shut?"

"Yes, sir."

"I'd appreciate it if you wouldn't mention what you saw tonight to anybody else."

"Yes, sir."

"She's a good woman, you know, and none of us is without weaknesses." Brother Feldman rubbed his chin. "My boy, I think you're going to find that most people try to hide their own sins by pointing out others' problems. I don't suppose you're perfect, are you?"

"No, sir."

He smiled. "I didn't think so."

The next afternoon after school I walked over to Sister Michaelis's home and raked the leaves off her lawn.

Sister Dahlberg showed up for church the first week in December. She sat next to my family. I never heard Sister Michaelis bear her "testimony" again.

5

Catch As Catch Can

It was about eight o'clock in the evening when the telephone rang in the records and identification division at the police station. "Records bureau," I answered.

"Break time," said Sergeant Olson. "Can one of you come sit at the desk for a few minutes?"

"Sure," I said. I hung up the phone and called out to our shift supervisor. "Ernie needs someone to give him a break. Do you want me to go out to the desk?"

It was a slow night at the police station. Usually our shift supervisor relieved the desk sergeant, but since so little was going on, he decided to send me. The desk sergeant sat behind a huge raised desk in the main foyer of the police station. His job was to deal with people who came in off the street asking for information or help. He also handled telephone calls that weren't of an emergency nature. I had barely sat down when the phone rang.

"Desk sergeant," I answered. "Can I help you?"

"Ernest?" a woman's voice asked.

"I'm sorry, he's on a break. Can I help you?"

"I've been burglarized," she whispered loudly.

"Is the burglar still there?" I replied quickly.

"I don't think so," she whispered in return.

"Let me get some information from you," I said, pulling out a complaint form. "First, tell me your name."

There was a considerable pause before the woman replied, "This is Opal Poppenaux." She drew out the words—"Ooooh-Puhhl Pahhh-Penn-Oooooh."

"Could you spell your last name please?"

"Young man," she huffed, "just as it sounds. P-O-P-P-E-N-A-U-X." She ended with a snort.

"Thank you. Your address please."

She recited an address in the Avenues of Salt Lake City. She followed with her telephone number. "How soon can you have an officer here?"

"I'll call the dispatcher as soon as we finish with this report. I think you'll see someone within a very few minutes. Now, please tell me just what is missing."

"Ernest usually sends the officer first, then gets a list of what the burglar took."

Mrs. Poppenaux obviously had called the desk sergeant before. "I'm sorry, Mrs. Poppenaux—," I began.

"You can call me Opal," she interjected.

"Thank you, Mrs. Poppenaux, but could you just tell me what's missing?"

"Oh, all right. This time he took a pint of whipping cream and some strawberries."

My mouth dropped open. I was glad I was talking to her on the phone and not in person. I stifled a laugh. "Anything else?"

"Not this time. Just strawberries and cream. Now, how soon can you get an officer here?"

"He'll be on the way as soon as we finish our conversation. Is there anything else you'd like to tell me?"

"I can't imagine what," she said. "And please hurry. You never know when the burglar will return." Her voice sank to a shallow whisper during the last phrase. I heard her place the phone in its cradle.

I disconnected the phone and called the dispatcher. "I have a strange burglary," I said. "Strawberries and cream."

"Let me guess," said the dispatcher. "Mrs. Poppenaux, right?"

"I guess I've missed something. Is she a regular?" I asked.

"Only about twice a week for the last three months. I'll send a car up to quiet her fears."

A few minutes later Sergeant Olson returned from his break. "Any traffic while I was gone?"

"Just a burglary. A Mrs. Poppenaux."

Sergeant Olson let out a laugh. "What's missing this time, the rolling pin or her Bible?"

"Strawberries and cream. Tell me about her."

Sergeant Olson shifted into a more comfortable position in his swivel chair. "She's a lonely old lady who lives up on the Avenues. Nobody ever comes to visit her, so a couple of times each week she stages a burglary and gets a visit from a policeman."

"Does she really think she's had a burglary, or is she just doing it for the attention?"

Sergeant Olson shrugged his shoulders. "I don't know. I've never met her, but sometimes she calls and I just talk to her for a few minutes. She doesn't really sound crazy, more like she's just lonely, maybe a little afraid. Of course, I've never seen her. I've just talked to her on the phone. Who'd the dispatcher send?"

"I guess Bob. It's his district."

"Well," said Sergeant Olson, "why don't you make sure you take the report when he calls it in and you can ask him about . . . Oooh-pull." He mimicked her voice.

About half an hour later Officer Bob Armstrong walked into the records bureau. "Did you have the Poppenaux case?" I called out. He nodded. "Let me take it." I sat down across the desk from him to take the report.

Officer Armstrong checked the information on the top of the complaint report and then dictated the following:

"Arrived at the above address at 8:08 p.m. After ringing the front doorbell, I could hear multiple dead bolts being opened. After approximately two minutes the front door was opened. Mrs. Opal Poppenaux identified herself as the person who had called in the burglary. I asked what, if anything, was missing. Mrs. Poppenaux indicated the following: one cup of strawberries, one pint of whipping cream. Both of the above items had been taken from the refrigerator."

Officer Armstrong had only the slightest hint of a smile on his lips. He continued.

"I began a room-by-room search with Mrs. Poppenaux. Due to the circumstances, I did not call for a backup unit. The missing strawberries and whipping cream were found in the shower in the bathroom. Neither item seemed damaged, although both were quite warm.

"Mrs. Poppenaux indicated that she must have frightened the burglar in the act of stealing the above items and he fled, leaving the items behind. We searched her house thoroughly and determined that no burglar was in the house. We completed the search at approximately 8:24 p.m. Although the victim invited me to stay longer in case the burglar returned, I assured her that all of her doors and windows were secured and she could lock the front door behind me after I left.

"Since the allegedly stolen items have been recovered, there is no evidence of breaking and entering, and no other evidence of the burglar was found, there probably does not need to be a follow-up investigation."

I finished typing the report and handed it to Officer Armstrong to sign. He read it and signed it. "Tell me about her," I said.

"Not much to tell. She's an old lady who's about half a bubble off level. Tonight was pretty easy. I found the strawberries and cream in about ten minutes. The other night she had really hidden her ceramic cat. It took me about forty-five minutes to find it."

"Where?"

"In the vegetable crisper in her refrigerator. I don't know whether she's just a lonely, scared old lady, or whether she really believes she has burglars. Anyway, I wish we could solve the problem. It's getting so it takes too much time off the street to help her find the things she's hidden around the house." He stood up and waved good-bye.

Since it was such a slow night, I had time to search back through the burglary complaints. Mrs. Poppenaux's call that night was her forty-first burglary in the last three months. The items ranged from silverware to toothpaste. My curiosity began to get the best of me.

The next afternoon as I left the university and headed to work at the police station, I decided to drive past Mrs. Poppenaux's house. I had to detour only a couple of blocks. It stood on the Avenues northeast of downtown Salt Lake City. It appeared to be a turn-of-the-century home that fit in with the surrounding neighborhood. An enormous maple tree grew in the front yard, partially obscuring the house from the roadway. On impulse I pulled over to the curb and got out of my car. I climbed the sandstone stairway to the front door and rang the doorbell. I heard the doorbell ring and then a moment later a voice through the door. "Yes?"

"Mrs. Poppenaux? I'm from the police department, here about last night's burglary."

"They've already found my strawberries," she said. "What do you want?"

"I'm just doing a follow-up," I lied. "Can I talk to you for a moment?"

I heard the first of several dead-bolt locks being opened. A few minutes later the door opened and revealed Opal Poppenaux. She was about seventy years of age, ramrod straight, with piercing black eyes in a heavily powdered face. Her silver-white hair was pulled back into a severe bun on the back of her head. A pair of eyeglasses dangled from a gold chain around her neck. She was dressed in a blue flowered housecoat and bright red slippers. In her left hand she held a newspaper, and as the door opened, she pulled a bottle of ketchup from a pocket in the housecoat with her right hand. "Let me see some identification," she barked.

Since I was in uniform, that seemed like an unusual request, but I pulled my wallet from my pocket and showed her my identification card. Opal relaxed, and invited me into her house. As I entered, a wave of mildew and mold swept over me. She walked to a wooden stool next to the fireplace, sat down, and gestured with the bottle of ketchup for me to have a seat on the couch. As I lowered myself onto the couch I knew I had made a mistake. The couch was soaking wet. The minute I sat down, my shirt and pants were likewise soaked. I jumped back to my feet. "Your couch is all wet!" I said loudly.

She leaned toward me and in a conspiratorial voice said, "I have to wash the ashes off. They're radioactive, you know. The Russians fly over and drop them every day." I looked through the archway into her kitchen and saw a garden hose coiled on the floor. I began to wish I hadn't decided to visit Mrs. Poppenaux.

"Well, have you discovered anything else missing? Besides the strawberries and cream, I mean." I could feel the wetness seeping through my underclothing.

"I think maybe he ate a few of the grapes, but I forgot to count them after dinner, so I can't be sure," she whispered. Her eyes shifted around the room. "You have to be careful what you say. They've bugged my house."

I edged toward the front door. "I guess that's about all, then. Thank you, Mrs. Poppenaux."

She glided across the room to the front door. "I'm sure they'll be back. I'll be calling you." She slammed the door, and I heard the dead bolts firing into place.

That night when Officer Armstrong came in to make a report, I mentioned I'd dropped by Mrs. Poppenaux's house out of curiosity. "Turn around," he said. My trousers were still a little wet from the encounter with her couch. "Sat down, didn't you?" He laughed. "Well, what did you think of Opal?"

"A little crazy, I guess, but scared and lonely. I'm sure we're going to have calls up there every other night, unless something changes."

"Well," said Bob, "if you can think of a solution, let me know. I'm getting tired of spending half my time at her house." He signed his report and walked out to his patrol car.

I walked out to the desk sergeant and told Sergeant Olson what I'd learned about Opal. I asked him to let me know if and when the next burglary occurred. Two nights passed before he mentioned casually, "Oh, by the way, Mrs. Poppenaux was burglarized tonight. This time her sunglasses were taken. They found them in the oven. It's too bad we can't catch the burglar." He laughed.

When Officer Armstrong came in to file his report, I said to him, "Bob, what if the burglar got caught?"

"You're crazy, man. There isn't any burglar. The old lady's just hiding the stuff herself and either forgetting where she put it or just calling out for some company."

"I know that and you know that, but what if the next time she reports a burglary the burglar gets caught? What do you think would happen?"

Bob shrugged his shoulders and smiled at me. "I'm willing to find out. Off the record, of course."

"Of course."

Two nights later the phone rang in the records bureau. Officer Armstrong was on the line. "Can you take a break and meet me at Opal's? Someone has stolen three boxes of Jell-O."

I checked out on a break and made the five-minute drive to the Poppenaux residence. Officer Armstrong was waiting in his patrol car. I parked around the corner and retrieved a black turtleneck sweater from the trunk of my car. With a black mask and slouch cap in place, I made my way carefully to Opal's front lawn. While I hid in the shadow of the maple tree, Officer Armstrong rang the bell.

The locks were undone, one by one, and finally the front door opened. "Come in, Officer," said Opal. Bob Armstrong entered the house and made sure the door stayed open behind him.

"What was taken this time, Mrs. Poppenaux?" he asked.

"Three boxes of Jell-O—one lime and two cherry, I think," she replied.

I heard the voices growing fainter as they moved toward the kitchen. Quickly I ran up the steps to the porch and stepped into the house. "I don't know why they don't leave me alone," said Opal from the kitchen in frustration. The two of them started back into the front room. Suddenly Bob turned on his flashlight and shined it in my direction. Bathed for a moment in the beam of his light, I paused, then bolted from the house.

"Stop, thief!" cried Officer Armstrong as he raced out of the house. He cleared the front steps in a single bound and tackled me on the front lawn. Without much of a scuffle he handcuffed the burglar and dragged him to his feet. "There, Mrs. Poppenaux," he said exultantly, "we've caught the filthy scoundrel. I don't think you'll be bothered by burglars anymore!"

Opal fairly danced on the front porch. She clapped her hands in excitement as Bob dragged me to the patrol car and shoved me into the backseat. "Now, lock up behind you," he said to Opal as he climbed into the front seat of his car. Opal walked quickly back into the house and shut the door.

Bob drove me around the corner to my car and unlocked the cuffs while we chuckled together. I was only five minutes late getting back to the station from my break.

Three weeks later Sergeant Olson stuck his head into the records bureau. "Remember Opal Poppenaux? I haven't heard from her for some time, but she just called to tell me her burglar had a brother. He's stolen a pound of hamburger."

6

Try to Remember

"Mother's finally gotten around to telling her life story," began Mr. Buchanan. "I'm wondering if you would like to earn an extra fifty dollars by typing it for her."

"I'd be delighted to help her with it, Mr. Buchanan. Just what exactly do you need done?" Frank Buchanan had called me at home the night before and asked if he could meet me after school. Now he sat with his briefcase on his lap. He unlatched the case and opened it. Inside were a number of cassette tapes.

"Well, we've been trying to get Mother to write her life story for years. She always said she'd get around to it when she got old. She's nearly ninety, and Dad and I finally talked her into telling us her story. We bought a tape recorder and she's been telling us about her life. It's a little disjointed—she jumps from year to year—but we thought if you'd transcribe it, we could organize it a bit and make a copy for each of her children, grandchildren, maybe even the great-grandchildren. I have no idea how long it will take you, but Dad and I thought we'd offer you fifty dollars and see if you'd be interested."

"I can give it a try. How soon do you need it done?"

"We'd like to finish it before she dies," he chuckled, "but she seems to be going strong. I guess there's really no hurry. Just whenever you can get to it." He removed a stack of tapes from his briefcase and placed them on my desk. Then he removed another stack, and another. I counted the tapes. There were thirty of them.

"Looks like quite a life," I said, gesturing toward the tapes.

"Mom's hearing and eyesight are going, but her memory's as sharp as it ever was. I haven't heard all of the tapes, but the ones I've listened to . . . well, she seems pretty thorough in her recollections." He rose from his chair and walked out of my room.

As I placed the tapes in a cardboard box, I noticed they were numbered. That evening I placed tape number one in my tape recorder and punched the play button. "I was born on May fifth, 1880, just outside the town of Bountiful in the territory of Deseret," came the raspy voice from the speakers. "The midwife, I think a woman by the name of Moss, delivered me at my grandmother's home. She said I was the most beautiful baby she had ever delivered. At least that's what my mother wrote in her journal. No wonder I grew up to be such a beautiful woman." There was a scratchy, wheezing laugh.

I thought of Grandma Buchanan, all four feet nine inches of her. By the time I first met her, five years before, she had lost all of her teeth and most of her hair. Her eyes were clouded and her mouth surrounded with so many wrinkles that it appeared she was perpetually sucking on a pickle. Her hands were knobbed and twisted with arthritis, and she moved in a painful shuffle when she walked.

By the end of the evening I finished transcribing about half of one side of the first tape. Most of what Grandma Buchanan recorded she had read from her mother's journals. She admitted that she didn't remember much of the first five years of her life. The exception was an incident involving the next-door neighbor boy who had pulled her pigtails during a church outing. She chased him, slipped on some greasewood, and ripped a hole in the knee of one stocking. "I got even with him, though," she recalled. "Married him fourteen years later and made him buy me a new pair of stockings."

The following night we reached 1896. Grandma Buchanan stated, "And then one day Utah became a state." Although I continued transcribing until I reached the end of the tape, there was no further mention of statehood. The next afternoon I called Frank Buchanan and mentioned this rather abbreviated handling of what I thought was a fairly significant event.

"Do you think your mother would let me interview her? There are a number of parts of her story that I'm sure make sense to her, but I'm a little confused as to what she's trying to say. I'd be considerate of her time, but I really think some things need to be fleshed out."

"I'll ask her," said Frank. Later that night he called and said his mother would be happy to talk to me.

The following afternoon when school was out I drove to the Buchanan home. The house was a fairly small rectangular brick building with a chimney at each end. I parked in the gravel driveway and walked to the front door. Grandpa Buchanan met me at the door. "Come in, come in. We've been expecting you." He ushered me into the parlor of their home. There, seated in her rocking chair, was the matriarch of the family.

I gently took her proffered hand and then sat on the couch. After a few minutes of idle chitchat, I showed her the sheaf of papers I had transcribed from her tapes. She seemed pleased. Then I said, "Mrs. Buchanan, I came to talk to you about your statement about statehood, or, more specifically, your lack of information. Could you tell me about what happened?" The sunlight played on her withered hands while we waited for a few moments.

"That's not a very happy memory," she said. "Father practiced plural marriage, you know, and he had to hide from the marshals. I think I was about twelve when he left for nearly six weeks. We had hay to harvest, and all of us had to work all day long in the field. I remember my tongue getting so dry and thick in my mouth that it split and bled, but we couldn't take time even to go to the well—we had a free-flowing well just west of Onion Street—we couldn't even go get a drink, 'cause we were afraid it was going to rain on the cut hay and make it mold.

"We worked from daybreak to sunset. I had to wear this terrible long homespun wool dress. It came clear down to my wrists, and I'd sweat so much that my dress would cling to me and the dust would mix with the sweat and form caked mud on the back of my neck. There were always alfalfa leaves that stuck to you too, along with the dust from the hay. At night, when we'd finally quit, my stockings would be so wet with sweat that I could wring muddy water from them."

Grandma Buchanan was looking up at the corner of the room above my head. We were back in 1893, and the coolness of their parlor had been replaced with the heat of the burning summer sun. Suddenly she said, "Do you ever watch Western movies? John Wayne?"

"Sometimes," I replied.

"One thing always bothered me about 'em. Nobody ever gets dirty. They ride in those covered wagons all day, and they all have clean hands and clothes when they're fixing their evening meal. I can tell you that's not right. The worst thing of my young life was dust and dirt. President Young said this place would blossom like a rose, but even roses are planted in the dirt." While she was talking she slid forward to the edge of her chair. Now she slid back. "Judge Zane was so bitter toward plural marriage. So bitter. Then came the end of polygamy, the Manifesto, and suddenly he changed his tune. I guess I ought to feel better toward him, but he was so bitter, so bitter.

"Father belonged to the People's Party, you know. That was sort of a Church party. The ones who opposed it belonged to the Liberal Party. I think the Church knew they were going to have to become part of national politics. We had two Apostles—I forget which ones—come to conference up in the Tabernacle and preach about having to be Republicans or Democrats. Father, of course, didn't want to have anything to do with the Republicans, 'cause they were responsible for most of the anti-polygamy legislation. I think everybody was going to join the Democrats. President Cleveland was a Democrat, and he signed the paper that made Utah a state. I heard that some bishops even divided the congregation in two and made one half Democrats and the other half Republicans. Didn't happen in our ward, though. There was a lot of commotion surrounding statehood and politics. One of Father's friends was an Apostle by the name of Thatcher. He had some disagreements, stemming from political matters, with the other General Authorities and ended up being dropped from the Quorum of the Twelve. I didn't get real involved in that, but it did sour my memories about statehood." She paused and wrinkled her mouth for a moment or two.

"Now, a year later, of course, that was quite the celebration. We travelled into Salt Lake to the Tabernacle for the first anniversary. There was red, white, and blue bunting strung all along the balconies. They had ribbons from the center of the ceiling running over to the walls, flags everywhere, and a great big star on the front of the Tabernacle organ pipes. That was a happier memory, much happier."

While she was talking, her voice grew softer. She heaved an enormous sigh. "Much happier." Her eyes closed and she drifted off to sleep. Grandpa Buchanan had already drifted off. I rose quietly and let myself out of the house.

During the following six weeks I followed Emma Buchanan as she moved south to Salina to help with a sheep herd, north to Brigham City to help with the fruit crop, and back to Bountiful. I typed the remembrances of her marriage, the birth of each of her ten children, and the loss of five of those children, three to disease and two to war.

I learned her homemade ice cream recipe—fresh peach was her favorite. I travelled back sixty years to sit with her beneath the trees that she and her husband planted and watered by hand. She helped me see the first automobile drive through town. "It was red, wasn't it, honey? With a little gold trim?"

"If you say so, dear," was Grandpa's reply. He looked in my direction and mouthed the word, "Black." I could tell this discussion had been held before.

"And it wasn't much later that we saw an airplane. An ungainly thing with sticks and struts and canvas, but it flew . . . it flew."

World War I came and went on tapes seven and eight. The Great Depression began on tape twelve. "Daddy had bought a telescope to look at the stars. We used to point it up at the hill and watch the men cutting terraces with the government work projects. That was after the floods in the thirties. We felt very fortunate because we grew most of our own food. I don't think our children ever went hungry. Always own enough property to grow a garden," she counselled.

World War II was neatly covered in two sentences: "The Japanese bombed Pearl Harbor and drew us into the war. We lost two sons."

I debated whether to try to get more information, and at last visited again. "Is it too painful to talk about the loss of your boys during the Second World War?" I asked.

There was a long pause while she gazed with her rheumy eyes toward the window. "No . . . time has a way of helping to heal old wounds. Bob—he was our baby—was always acting up. He got in a little trouble with the sheriff for putting .22 shells on the Bamberger train tracks. But when he shipped out to the Pacific, all his letters were pretty much the same. He was scared. I think he knew he wasn't going to come back, had a premonition. When I saw him off at the train station, I had this strange feeling I was saying good-bye to him for the last time. I cried all the way home. He was killed trying to get onto a beach. What do they call that, honey?"

"They were trying to secure a beach, Mother." The voice was tired and soft.

"Ron was shot just outside of Paris. They both came home in flag-draped coffins. A part of my life, my heart, was buried with them. You know, they've never aged in my memory. They're still the same vibrant young men who went off to serve their country. Isn't that funny? All of my other children have aged. They've gotten bald and paunchy, but not Bob and Ron." Her voice trailed off. "They're still young men. Maybe they keep a little piece of me young, too." A tear slid slowly down her cheek. "Freedom is so precious and so hard to keep. I'd like to say I don't begrudge their loss, but I do. Fighting seems like such a useless thing to do. He knew what He was saying when He said, 'Blessed are the peacemakers.' "

The sun was setting, leaving the room in shadows as I left.

President Roosevelt died, Truman was sworn in, and the atom bomb exploded in the next few tapes. "I remember I was standing at the kitchen sink washing some dishes. I'd been making cookies, chocolate chip, when they announced on the radio that the president had been shot. I remember putting the cookies in the cookie jar and thinking, 'Not in America.' Then that night we saw the pictures on television. I remember saying to Dad, 'He's so young and she's so pretty.' "

Near the end of the tapes, Grandma Buchanan mentioned the birth of her first great-grandchild. I called Frank Buchanan and told him I was nearly finished. "When do you think you'll have them done?" he asked.

"If all goes well, I'll finish Saturday night."

"We're having a family get-together at Mom and Dad's Sunday evening. They've got a color television. Maybe you'd like to bring everything down there and explain to the whole family what you've done."

And so on Sunday, 20 July 1969, I delivered the final manuscript, 854 double-spaced legal pages, to Emma Buchanan and her family. She had weathered two world wars, Korea, and Vietnam. As I handed her son the typed copy, she said, "I don't really think it will be of interest to anyone."

She had been born in the days of the horse and buggy, had seen the first automobile and airplane come to Utah. From the television set we heard, "Tranquility Base. The *Eagle* has landed."

7

Walk in Faith

When my wife and I decided to move to the Navajo reservation so that we could teach school there, I was determined not to be an Ugly American. I scoured our local bookstore for books on the Navajo culture. I bought a copy of every book they had on the subject— both of them. I read them from cover to cover. Thus prepared, we packed our rental truck and began our trek.

It was nearly midnight when we pulled up in front of our apartment on the reservation. Our neighbor was waiting for us. Alerted by the lights of our truck, he greeted us and handed over the key to our apartment. We dragged a mattress from the truck and slept on the floor that night. The next morning we awoke to our first daylight view of our home. We were surrounded by the red soils and rocks of Navajo land. The only grass to be seen was a small patch behind our apartment and on the football field behind the high school across the street.

By noon our belongings were crammed into our small apartment. Our neighbors proved friendly and helpful. All of the apartments were occupied by schoolteachers. The rest of the faculty lived in house trailers half a mile away. We spent the afternoon returning the rental truck to Gallup, New Mexico, nearly a hundred miles away.

The Church of Jesus Christ of Latter-day Saints provides religious instruction during the week for young Church members on the reservation. When it was discovered that I was going to be teaching math and science at the high school, I was approached by a man representing the Church Educational System about teaching fourth-grade boys two days a week after school. And so as the school year began I met with my six "Johnny Braves" every Tuesday and Thursday for an hour. We used a classroom in the little branch building. Four of the boys lived within walking distance of the church. The other two lived up the canyon. Often I drove these two to their homes.

Billy lived with his grandmother in a hogan nearly two miles up the wash. For the first two weeks I saw nothing of his grandmother. I dropped Billy off in front of his grandmother's hogan, waved good-bye, and left. The third Tuesday, Billy's grandmother, Yahnbah Begay, was waiting in front of the hogan when we drove up. Billy picked up a well-worn basketball and began throwing the ball toward a hoop nailed to a post near the shade shelter, while his grandmother and I tried to speak to each other. I had found a man who was trying to teach me the language, but my knowledge of Navajo was minimal and her command of English was not much better. She pointed at Billy and at me and smiled. I smiled back.

Thursday when I arrived Yahnbah Begay met me in front of her hogan. In her hand she had a copy of the *Navajo Times*. The *Times* was a newspaper printed by the tribe. It arrived at the trading posts on Thursdays. Mrs. Begay spoke to Billy in Navajo.

Then Billy said to me, "She wants to know if you can read Navajo."

Every week the *Navajo Times* printed a column in phonetic Navajo. This column was interesting for several reasons. First, Navajo is a non-written language. Two Catholic priests by the names of Young and Morgan developed a written phonetic language, and the column was written in the language they'd developed. Second, I didn't know any of the non-English-speaking Navajos who could read the column. The only people I knew who could read the column were people, like me, who were trying to learn the Navajo language and had learned the Young and Morgan system of phonetics. I could read it; I just didn't understand very much of what I was reading.

"Tell her, Billy, I will try to read the *Diné Bisaadish*." Billy translated for his grandmother. She offered the newspaper to me. I turned to the column in question and began to read. Mrs. Begay nodded her head frequently and muttered occasionally as I struggled with the unfamiliar Navajo words. When I finished I handed the newspaper back to her. Yahnbah Begay was dressed in a maroon velvet blouse and a black full skirt, the traditional dress copied from the officers' wives at Fort Sumner following the long march a century before. Around her neck was a silver squash blossom necklace. She smiled a broad smile at me. I could see that several of her teeth were missing. "*Hahgoneh*, Yahnbah Begay," I said as I stood to leave.

"Good-bye," she replied.

For the next several weeks we followed the ritual of reading the Navajo column together every Thursday. Little by little my Navajo vocabulary was improving and I was beginning to understand some of the words as I read them.

One Sunday in late November the branch president of our little congregation asked me to step into his office after sacrament meeting. "You're pretty good friends with Sister Begay, aren't you?"

"Well, I take her grandson home after our Johnny Brave class on Tuesdays and Thursdays," I replied. "On Thursdays I usually read her the Navajo language column from the *Navajo Times*. That's about as far as our friendship has gotten. Why?"

"Do you know her daughter, Sarah? She's probably a granddaughter, or niece, but she lives with Sister Begay. Do you know which one she is?"

Whenever I'd been at the Begay hogan the only two people I'd seen were Yahnbah Begay and Billy. "I don't think I've ever seen her, President. Is something wrong?"

"No, no, nothing like that. Sarah's been going to school at BYU. When she came home she sent in her mission papers. She just got her mission call from Church headquarters and she's going to serve over on the other side of the reservation. I was just wondering if you could talk to Sister Begay for me and let her know that there are many people in the branch who want to help support Sarah on her mission. It's going to cost about seventy-five dollars a month, and I've got more than enough contributions to cover her expenses. It's kind of hard for me to talk to Sister Begay, not knowing the language. I hoped you'd talk to her for me. What do you say?"

"I'd be happy to give her your message, President.

I imagine she'll be grateful. I don't think she has much of anything to help support Sarah. I'm not sure how she survives herself. All she has is a little garden and a small flock of sheep. I'll talk to her on Tuesday."

"Thanks. Let her know we are happy for the opportunity to help."

Tuesday afternoon I drove Billy home. Yahnbah Begay, dressed in her maroon blouse and black skirt, was sitting in the sun, absorbing its warmth. "I'm going to need your help translating, Billy," I said as he started to get out of the car. "I need to talk to your grandmother."

"I'll get her," he said, and ran to where she was sitting outside the shade shelter. I waited a few moments, as was the custom, then got out of the car and walked to where the two were waiting.

"*Yah-et-eeh*," I said. She returned my greeting. "Grandmother," I began, "the branch president has asked me to talk with you about Sarah's mission." Billy translated as best he could. "He has asked me to tell you there are many friends who would like to help pay the money Sarah will need to stay on her mission." As Billy began to translate, Yahnbah suddenly sat bolt upright and turned to look me straight in the eye.

She fired off a few sentences in rapid Navajo. Billy translated, "She says, don't you want her to get the blessings?" He looked at the ground by his feet and drew a box in the dirt with the toe of his boot. "She says she will take care of Sarah." Then he looked at me. "I don't think she wants to be rude, but she doesn't want to have any help, OK?"

"Billy, ask her how she will pay the money each month. Tell her I don't want to be rude either, but I am curious where she will get seventy-five dollars each month." He began to translate, haltingly. Sister Begay listened to his words, then turned to me and spoke very softly.

My Johnny Brave translated, "It is arranged with the trading post. She will give them a sheep each month and they will send the money to Sarah." His eyes grew large as he finished speaking. He looked at the sheep in the rude corral. We spoke together for a few more minutes, and I promised to tell the branch president that she would take care of the mission expenses. As I walked back to my car I looked in the corral at the small flock of sheep. I counted them—one ram and seventeen ewes. Sarah's mission call was for eighteen months.

I drove to the branch president's trailer behind the church and told him of my conversation with Sister Begay. "She has eighteen sheep, President. Maybe we ought to put the contributions into an account to buy her some more sheep when Sarah is released."

"Stubborn old woman," he said.

"I guess," I replied. "She seems pretty set in her ways. I don't think we ought to risk offending her."

In sacrament meeting, Sarah spoke about her desire to go on a mission. She was a beautiful young woman, radiant with the knowledge that she was doing what she and the Lord wanted done. When she finished, Yahnbah Begay made her way to the pulpit. In Navajo she told how proud she was of Sarah and then explained that she would take care of Sarah while she was on her mission. "The Lord promises blessings if you follow his commandments," she said.

The first Tuesday in December I dropped Billy off at his hogan. There were sixteen ewes in the corral. I visited the trading post on the way home and bought some fresh mutton.

65

On Thursday, after reading the newspaper, I asked Sister Begay if she had heard from Sarah. A bright smile illuminated her face. She walked into her hogan, and returned with a letter from her missionary. I read it out loud and Billy translated for his grandmother. Sarah was doing well. She had a marvellous missionary companion from Tuba City, and they were very busy teaching the gospel.

In January there were fifteen ewes. In February, fourteen. The branch president asked me to approach Yahnbah Begay again about some financial help from the branch. "Sister Begay," I said to her, "the branch president asked me to see if you would let him help pay some of the money for Sarah's mission."

"*Doh-dah,*" she replied immediately when Billy finished his translation. "No, I will pay for Sarah myself. It is my duty. It is my right. It is my blessing! Don't rob me of my blessings!"

Billy cleared his throat. "I don't think she wants any help. Please don't have me ask her again. OK?"

I took the message back to the branch president. "Stubborn old woman," he said. "She's not going to have a sheep left by the time Sarah gets home. I wish she'd let us help her now. It's going to be really hard when she has to swallow her pride and ask for some help from the Church next year."

In March there were thirteen ewes. Each Sunday Sister Begay came to church and, through Billy, told us what a fine job Sarah was doing on her mission. The branch president listened and shook his head.

Then came the first Sunday in April. The day was clear and cool. A smattering of wooly white clouds floated slowly across the blue bowl of the sky. We had no organ in our small chapel, but Sister Anderson began playing prelude music on the piano. Nearly all of the twenty-five regular members of the congregation were standing outside the church talking before sacrament meeting began. I glanced up the dirt path that led to the wash and saw Billy and Sister Begay hurrying as fast as her ancient legs could carry her. They were raising a cloud of dust as they hurried along. She was shouting something and waving her right hand in the air. Her left hand held up the hem of her ample black skirt. Finally, over the sound of the piano, I could hear her voice. *"Dabeh nakii, dabeh nakii,"* she was shouting over and over. "Two sheep, two sheep."

I became alarmed. Had Sarah incurred some extra expenses that required Yahnbah Begay to sacrifice two sheep instead of one? The branch president turned to me. "What's she saying? Can you make it out?"

"She's saying, 'Two sheep.' I wonder if something's happened to Sarah."

"Maybe she'll let us give her some help now," he replied.

And then suddenly, breathlessly, they were there. Billy explained. Every one of Sister Begay's pregnant ewes had had twin lambs—and this from a breed of sheep whose ewes always have a single lamb. There were enough to supply the trading post each month until the lambs could be weaned from their mothers.

When Sarah returned from her mission, Sister Begay had a flock of thirty sheep.

8

Do unto Others

"Would you do me a favor?" asked my friend Thomas. "I have this couple I've been trying to counsel, and they just won't listen to me. They both know you. I think you taught them both about fifteen years ago. Anyway, they said they'd like to talk with you. What do you think? Willing to give it a shot?"

Thomas and I graduated together from high school. In my yearbook from my senior year, Thomas—always Thomas, never Tom—wrote nearly half a page. I'm sure I did the same in his. We pledged undying friendship, and did see each other a couple of times that summer before we began university life. We went to different schools, and our lives parted. Nearly twenty years passed, and then we bumped into each other in our local supermarket.

Thomas was moving back to our hometown. I'd

returned five years before. We stood by the dairy case and tried to catch up on the last twenty years. He brought his family to our house for hamburgers that night, and we helped them carry boxes into their new home. Although we lived only four blocks apart, we were in different wards, or congregations, of The Church of Jesus Christ of Latter-day Saints. In our area every half dozen wards were organized into a stake. We even lived in different stakes, since the road in front of my family's house was the dividing line between the two stakes.

We rekindled our friendship, and every few weeks our families did something together. Then Thomas was called as the bishop of his ward. With the time demands of his calling, our get-togethers became fewer and farther apart. The following spring I was called as bishop in my ward. The meetings between our families became even less frequent.

And now came a phone call with the request that I help him counsel a couple in his ward. "For you, anything. Tell me who they are and what the problem is."

Thomas asked me if I remembered Wally Franklin. "Of course," I said. "Who could forget him? He was probably the brightest kid I ever taught."

"He thought you might remember him. He married Gayle Johnson about three or four years ago. They have a little girl about a year old. They're just kind of, well, tired of being married. I've tried talking to them, but they think I'm too old-fashioned or something. Anyway, they both mentioned your name, and I thought it was worth a shot. I'll tell them you're willing to see them. When's a good time?"

I checked my calendar and suggested some possible times. Thomas said he'd have the Franklins get back to me. Ten minutes later the phone rang again, and Gayle Franklin asked if she could visit with me the following Sunday evening.

Gayle Johnson, I thought. *Cheerleader, full of fun, never too dedicated to her studies but enough that she was eligible to stay on the cheerleading squad.* I hadn't thought about her in years, but my mind went back to basketball games in which she led the team onto the court with a yell followed by five or six back flips. She was the stereotypic cheerleader—frothy, fun, and full of energy. The high point of her high school experience seemed to revolve around decorating lockers and delivering cookies or cakes to team members before the "big game." She changed boyfriends as often as she changed shoes. Each one deserved her full attention for at least two weeks. Then she moved on to the next one.

One day stuck out in my memory—the day we dissected sharks in my science class. Gayle took one look at the dogfish shark lying in its dissecting pan, sniffed its preservative, and said, "Ooh, I can't touch that thing. It smells terrible." She squeezed her nose between thumb and forefinger and pretended to faint. However, after putting on rubber gloves, she did the most careful dissection I had seen all year. Every cut was done with surgical precision and every organ carefully isolated and identified. When it was time to clean up, Gayle carefully wrapped her shark in wet cheesecloth. "How much more time do we get?" she asked.

"Tomorrow," I replied.

"Can I come in after school and work on it? I don't think I can finish tomorrow." She worked nearly two hours after school. Many of her classmates had butchered their way to completion in the one class period. I began to wonder how much of Gayle's personality was an act.

Wally Franklin had been both a joy and a frustration. Wally absorbed information faster than a sponge absorbs water. He had a great memory and quick recall. Whenever we started a new concept in class, Wally reached the conclusion five minutes later. The rest of the class took considerably longer. Wally frequently became impatient with the rest of the class and wanted to move on. I began giving Wally individual research projects to do. He'd check in at the first of class, discover what we were doing that day, then slip out and go to the library.

There was only one question Wally ever missed on a test, and that created some controversy. While the class was studying the Krebs citric-acid cycle from our year-old textbook, Wally was studying it from an older book in the library. A slight correction in the cycle had been made between the two versions, and Wally missed the question on the test. He insisted that he be given credit, since he could document his answer. The fact that the "facts" had changed seemed irrelevant to Wally.

What in the world drew these two people together? I wondered. Frothy, little Gayle and tall, gangly Wally must have somehow drifted together. *Well,* I thought, *opposites attract.*

Sunday evening our Scoutmaster and one of my counselors were checking in money from the Scout sustaining membership drive, when Gayle Franklin appeared at my office door. They excused themselves and moved into the clerk's office.

"Would you give me just a moment, Gayle?" I asked. I closed the door and knelt beside my desk. *Help me, please, to be of help to this young couple.* I prayed a few more minutes, then rose and opened the door. Gayle extended her hand and shook mine.

"Thanks for seeing me, Mr. Sid— I guess that should be Bishop, shouldn't it?" She giggled nervously.

"Call me anything that feels comfortable, Gayle. It's been nearly ten years, hasn't it?"

"Actually, it's been about twelve, I think. Let's see . . ." And she began counting on her fingers the years since she graduated. "Oh, but I was a junior when I had your class, so that means . . ." She went on figuring. Gayle had been a pretty little cheerleader; she had blossomed into a beautiful young woman. As she sat in the chair across from me on the other side of the desk, it seemed that everything about her was as perfect as she could make it. Not a hair was out of place. There were no wrinkles on her face or in her clothing. She chattered on for a few minutes.

"Gayle, why don't you fill me in on what has happened in your life since I last saw you? I suppose quite a bit has happened in the last ten or eleven or twelve years, hasn't it?"

She inhaled a lungful of air and let out a mighty sigh. "After graduation I went off to school. I decided I wanted to be a doctor, but my grades weren't good enough and I couldn't get accepted into the pre-med program. They suggested I might transfer to another school that didn't have such tough requirements. Instead, I changed my major and went into sociology. I figured if I couldn't heal bodies, maybe I could help heal society. After a little while I discovered I really didn't like sociology, and I changed majors again. I probably changed my major a half dozen times in the next three years. While I was going to school I started working at a furniture store as a salesclerk. I discovered I had a flair for design. Pretty soon I was helping people decorate their houses. I dropped out of college and began my own little decorating company."

She paused and looked me straight in the face. "Pretty silly, huh?"

"Not at all. Are you still running your business?" I asked.

"Not really. Oh, I still do some decorating as a favor to a friend. But since we got married, Wally wants me to stay home. I don't do much of it anymore." She paused and seemed to take intense interest in the file cabinet in the corner of my office.

I took advantage of the pause. "How did you and Wally meet? Tell me about that."

"That was kind of funny. Wally's mother asked me to help her decorate for a wedding—Wally's older sister, maybe you remember Donna Jo?" I nodded that I remembered her. "I was there at their house, wearing some terrible outfit—Levi's and a sweatshirt, I think—when Wally walked in. I hadn't seen him since high school. He helped me with the decorations, and then about a week after the wedding he called me and asked me to go out to dinner. We dated for about a year and then got married." Her eyes were filling with tears. I offered her a box of Kleenex.

"Go on," I said.

Gayle dabbed at the tears with a tissue. "At first we were happy enough, and miserable, if you know what I mean. I guess it doesn't matter how long you date someone, you really don't know him until you get married." I nodded my head in agreement. "Do you know what our first fight was about? Whether you have to put a salad fork on the table if you're not having salad." She smiled through her tears. "Pretty stupid, huh?"

"Lots of people argue about where you squeeze

the toothpaste tube," I offered. "In retrospect these things seem pretty stupid, but at the time they appear to be major problems."

"I don't want to sound like we fought all the time. We really didn't. I think basically we were pretty happy. When I discovered I was pregnant, we were both overjoyed."

"Was it an easy pregnancy?" I asked.

"I had morning sickness twenty-four hours a day for nearly four months," she laughed. "Wally really pitched in and helped. When Alicia was born it seemed like our marriage was finally complete. But in the last year Wally has changed so much." Suddenly her face clouded and the tears began falling again. "I'm sorry," she choked through the sobs.

"Just take your time," I said. "Tell me about Wally, how he's changed."

A few minutes passed. "Well, when we were dating—I mean, here I was this dumb little girl, and he was the smartest kid I'd ever known. And he was really considerate. I mean, he'd open the door for me, and ask me what I wanted to do. And now . . . oh, I don't know. Now he's so demanding. I think he resents Alicia. He's always after me to leave her with a baby-sitter and she's only fourteen months old."

"How often do you leave her?" I asked.

"Never. She's not old enough yet. I wouldn't be here tonight if Wally weren't home with her."

"I see. What else has Wally done that makes you so unhappy?"

"He just never has time for me anymore. I don't know, I just don't think he wants to be married to me." She used up half a dozen more tissues. "He's just changed. I want more out of our marriage than I'm getting." She pushed herself from the chair. "I'm sorry. I've taken too much of your time. Thanks for listening."

I arose from my chair and walked around the desk. "Let me ask you two questions. Would you like to come and talk with me again? And do you think Wally would like to come?"

"Why? Do you think there's any way to save our marriage?" I heard the sound of defeat in her voice.

"Perhaps. Would you like to come again?" She nodded her head. "And Wally, do you think he'd come?" She shrugged her shoulders. "Please ask him," I said as I let her out the door.

I sank to my knees and offered another prayer for guidance. A feeling of peace came over me.

I was still working in my office an hour later, when the phone rang. "Bishop, this is Wally Franklin. If you have time, I'd like to talk to you." I assured him I'd take the time. Ten minutes later there was a knock on my door. It opened and in walked Wally.

"It's been a long time," I said, extending my hand. Wally shook it.

"Thanks for making time for me. I know you're not really our bishop and you really don't have to get involved, but I appreciate your taking time."

"My pleasure. How are you doing?"

"Pretty well, I guess. My engineering firm seems to have really taken off. We have more work than we can handle."

"I didn't know you were an engineer, but it doesn't surprise me. You were always such a good student."

"Thanks, Bishop. I really have fond memories of you. I don't think anybody else would have let me study on my own. And I'll never forget what you told me on graduation night."

I couldn't remember even seeing Wally at his graduation. In fact, after more than twenty years of commencements, I had trouble keeping them separate. "What was that, Wally?"

"You said, 'Wally, you can be anything you want to be.' I could tell you meant it. You know, I went off to college and met a lot of other really bright kids. There were times when I wanted to give it all up, and I'd remember what you said."

I didn't want to tell Wally that I'd said the same thing to thousands of students. Of course, it is pretty good advice.

"I went on a mission. Served in Brazil. Portuguese came pretty easy to me, but I really struggled with some of my companions. Some of them really didn't want to work. Maybe I was just being too hard on them. Anyway, I came home and finished school. I was hired by a good engineering firm. I stayed with them for about two years, then struck out on my own. We've done really well.

"Do you remember Gayle Johnson?" he asked. I nodded. "She came to my house to help decorate for my sister's wedding. Did you ever teach Donna Jo?"

"I remember her, Wally, but I didn't have her in class."

"Well, Gayle came to our house to decorate for Donna Jo's wedding. I've never felt really sure of myself around girls, especially really pretty ones like Gayle, but she asked me to help her with some of the decorations. After the wedding she told me she'd like to get together sometime. One thing led to another, and about a year later we got married in the Salt Lake Temple."

Temples are the most sacred places on earth to members of The Church of Jesus Christ of Latter-day Saints. In them, couples are married for time and eternity, not just for the probation of their mortal lives.

"We had all of her family and all of my family there. It was quite a gathering." Wally's somber face broke into just a hint of smile. "We've had a pretty good marriage," he conceded, "until this last year. Boy, has Gayle changed!"

"In what way, Wally?"

He examined the file cabinet with his eyes. "When Gayle was first pregnant—oh, I forgot to tell you, we have a little girl, Alicia—when Gayle was pregnant with her she was really sick and she let me help her. Gayle really likes to do things her way. You could tell if you visited our house. She usually won't let me help her with much of anything, but she was sick enough that she let me get in and help. But since Alicia was born, wow, I just have to get out of the way. I think Gayle would be happier if I weren't there. I thought temple marriages were supposed to be happy."

"Wally, we do a great job of preparing people to get married in the temple. We do a lousy job of preparing people to get married. Sometimes we focus so much on the temple, that we don't tell people what it's like to be married. Two people come to a marriage from different backgrounds. Each is convinced the whole world lives and behaves the way his or her family does. Then they get married and find they do things differently. Does that make sense?"

"Bishop, I know just what you mean. Do you know what our first argument was about?" I thought I did—something to do with a salad fork—but I shook my head. "Which side of the dresser was hers and which was mine. I grew up sharing a room with my brother, and I always had the left side of the dresser. Well, it turns out Gayle always had the left side of the dresser, too."

"How did you resolve it?" I asked.

"I gave in. I always have to give in. Gayle always wants things done her way. Period."

"You feel you always have to do things her way," I said.

"Yes! Well, most of the time. And she sends contradictory messages. I mean, she's always complaining about being stuck in the house with the baby, but she won't go anywhere without Alicia."

"You feel like you don't know what she really wants," I said.

"Bishop, I just feel like I ought to be getting more out of our marriage than I'm getting. Am I wrong?" He rose to go.

"Wally, let me ask you two questions. First, would you like to come and talk to me again, and second, do you think Gayle would come and talk to me?"

"I feel like I've taken too much of your time as it is," he said.

"Wally, would you like to come again?"

He thought for a moment. "If you think it would really do any good."

"What about Gayle? Do you think she'd come?"

He shrugged his shoulders. "I can ask."

After Wally left I called my friend Thomas. "I've just talked to the Franklins. What do you think their basic problem is?"

"Well, I don't think either one wants to change. They both want the other one to do all the changing. What do you think?"

"I think you've summed it up pretty well," I said. "I've asked them to come and see me again. I'll keep you posted."

For the third time that night I sank to my knees and asked for help. Although a feeling of peace came, I felt no clear direction as to what I could do.

Two days later Gayle called. "When would you have time to see me?"

"We'll be in the church for Mutual tonight," I said. "How about eight-thirty?"

"Fine. Wally will be home by then to take care of Alicia. See you then."

The joint activity involving the young men and women in my ward was ending. The kids were standing around the cultural hall eating Astro bars, a favorite frozen confection from a local drive-in, when I spotted Gayle in the foyer outside my office. I excused myself from the activity and went to greet her. "Just a minute, Gayle."

I entered my office and sank to my knees. *Father, I need help. These are two fine young people. Please, please help me know what I should say to help them.*

A powerful feeling of peace came over me. The Spirit whispered, *Love them.*

I invited Gayle into my office. After we seated ourselves, she said, "I understand Wally came to talk to you."

"That's right." Suddenly the words began to tumble from my mouth. "I've given quite a bit of thought to your situation since the other night. I could try to be gentle about this, but I'm going to be straightforward. I don't think your marriage has a chance in the world of succeeding." I sat upright in my chair. What in the world was I saying?

Her mouth dropped open. I saw tears well up in her eyes. "No chance? None at all?" she said.

"Gayle, I want to be your friend and I'm going to give you some advice. I think six months from now your marriage will be over. I've talked to Wally and I don't think he's willing to change at all. I want you to look ahead to what's going to happen at the time of the divorce. Wally is going to try to take Alicia away from you, and I think you need to protect yourself."

"No chance at all?" she said again.

"Gayle, listen to me. There's only one way you can protect yourself and your daughter. When Wally goes to court, he's going to paint you as the most uncooperative woman in the world. He's going to say that you are selfish and that you were totally unwilling to meet his needs or his desires. Do you understand what I'm saying?"

She nodded her head. "What do I do?"

"Gayle, what I'm going to ask you to do will be the hardest thing you've ever done in your life. I want you to promise me that whatever Wally asks you to do for the next six months, you'll do. Everything! Do you understand me?"

"Yes, but why?"

"Because when you go into court and you battle for the rights to this precious little girl of yours, your attorney is going to be able to say about you, 'She did everything this man asked her to do, and it's still not enough.' Do you love your little girl enough to do what I'm suggesting?"

"Oh yes. Are you sure I won't lose her?"

"Gayle, there are no guarantees, but I can tell you you'll have a much better chance of keeping her. There's one other part to this deal. You cannot, absolutely cannot, tell Wally what you're doing, or he'll be able to use it against you. Do you understand?"

Her eyes fell to the carpet. "I don't know if I can do it. It's going to be so hard."

"It's only for six months. You can do anything for six months, can't you?"

"I can," she said with resolve. "I'll do everything Wally asks me to do and I won't tell him a thing. I'm not going to let him get Alicia."

"Gayle, I'm serious about this. I want you to

promise me you'll do what I said. I'll always be here for you if you need to talk."

"I promise. I promise! Oh, I wish there were some other way."

I helped her to her feet and sent her out the door. The feeling of peace grew even stronger. Quickly I called their home. "Wally, can you come and see me as soon as Gayle gets home. I think we have to have a pretty serious conversation." He agreed to come. A few minutes later his car pulled into the parking lot, and soon there was a knock on my door. "Come in, Wally."

He burst into my office. "What's the matter, Bishop?"

"Have a seat, Wally." He seated himself slowly. "I have just finished talking with Gayle. I wish I had better news, but I'm convinced your marriage is over. Within six months you'll find yourself in divorce court and Gayle will be trying to take Alicia from you."

He leapt from his seat. "Not without a fight!"

"Wally, she's going to win because she's going to go into court and paint you as a man who is demanding and unwilling to change. She's going to tell the judge that you were totally unresponsive to her needs. I've been your friend for a long time, and I think you need to protect yourself. Here's what I'm asking you to do. For the next six months, whenever Gayle asks you to do anything, you do it. Treat her like a queen. Then when your court date arrives you can show that you have done everything in your power to keep your wife happy. Do you understand?"

As I spoke, he sank slowly into his chair. "You're right," he said. "She's going to make it look like I'm the one to blame. Bishop, you've got a deal. From this moment I pledge to do everything and anything my wife wants. What else?"

"Wally, you can't tell her what you are doing. You can never let it slip that you are doing this to prove you are a worthy husband and father, or she'll bring it up in court and it will explode in your face! Do you understand?"

He stood up quickly. "I understand perfectly. She's going to get a perfect husband and never know what it's all about. Thanks for looking out for me, Bishop." He walked quickly to the door.

"Wally, I'm always here if you need to talk."

He climbed into his car and drove away. I sank to my knees. *Well done,* whispered the Spirit.

I called my friend Thomas. "I tried to work out a solution. I think you'll need to keep a pretty careful eye on the Franklins." He agreed.

I heard nothing more from him or the Franklins for nearly four months, when I bumped into Gayle at the grocery store. "How are you two getting along?"

"Bishop, you were wrong. I took your advice, but Wally and I aren't getting a divorce. I can't imagine why you thought our marriage was at an end. He's the most considerate husband and father I've ever seen. He treats me like a queen."

I'm sure Wally feels he is married to one. The Lord works in mysterious ways, his wonders to perform.

9

Because I Have Been Given Much

I questioned why the Jenkins family bought the old Whipple home as much as anyone. Four or five years before, Virginia Jenkins had suffered a stroke that left her confined to a wheelchair and without speech. The Whipple home had five bedrooms on its two floors and a large yard that required constant care. The Jenkinses were both in their seventies when they moved in. It seemed to me to be too large for their needs. But move in they did.

Patrick Jenkins stood over six feet tall. He had a thatch of snow white hair that seemed always to be falling forward over his left eye. He stood ramrod straight and spoke in quick, clipped words. His standard outfit consisted of a blue workshirt, sleeves rolled to the elbows, and a pair of well-worn overalls. The day they moved in he began constructing a ramp to the front door. He worked with the speed and skill of a practiced carpenter. By evening he was able to wheel his wife up the ramp and into their living room.

Virginia Jenkins sat strapped to her wheelchair. Although she could not speak, she obviously understood everything that was going on. She had lost the use of her left arm, but her right hand was constantly in motion, pointing to one thing or another in the room. She and her husband seemed to communicate without words, or at least without words from her. Patrick was always chatting away. "Well, Mother, I think we've fixed this ramp up pretty good. What do you think? Let's give it a try. Grab on, Mother, and we'll try to keep from bucking you out." And up the ramp they went.

When they moved in, a huge number of people showed up to help them. I offered a hand if it was needed, but Patrick said, "I think we have everything pretty much under control, don't we, Mother! But thanks for your offer."

"Your family?" I asked, indicating the army of helpers.

He paused for a minute and surveyed the crew. "Yes . . . our family."

Within a week the whole neighborhood was familiar with the Jenkinses' routine. At eight o'clock every morning the front door opened and out came Virginia Jenkins in her wheelchair. Patrick pushed her down the ramp and around the house to the backyard. There he parked her in the shade of a huge chestnut tree while he worked in the garden. Every few minutes he came to her side and asked if she needed anything. Usually she shook her head, but occasionally she nodded her head and then Patrick began his guessing game. "Do you want a drink, Mother?" She'd either shake or nod her head. If he was wrong, Patrick continued, "Are you hungry, Mother? Do you need to be moved? Are you too cold? Are you too hot?" On and on he'd go until he guessed Virginia's need.

Throughout the week various members of the family appeared at their home. From my vantage point across the street, I began to recognize some of their children. Three or four times a week a blue Honda pulled up and a dark-complexioned woman of considerable bulk climbed out. She'd walk around the house to the back yard and spend a few minutes before she reappeared, climbed into her little car, and drove away. Not quite so frequently a bright red Chevrolet pulled up and a short, blond woman with two small children emerged.

The Jenkinses had a garden area in their back yard about forty feet square. The Whipples had not planted anything in it for several years. One Saturday morning I watched Patrick push Virginia around the house and a few minutes later saw him carry an armload of weeds to the garbage can on the curb. I walked across the road and into their backyard. Virginia sat in the shade of the chestnut tree while Patrick sliced away at the weed patch with a scythe. When he spotted me, he laid his scythe against the fence and walked toward me. He pulled off his leather work glove and shook my hand. "What a pleasure to have you visit Mother and me," he said. "It will give me a well-needed break." Virginia smiled at me and waved her right hand. I took it in mine and shook it gently. She squeezed my hand firmly.

"I have a tiller," I said. "Could I be of assistance? I'd be happy to till that garden area for you."

Virginia's face lit up. Patrick said, "Are you sure? I wouldn't want to be a burden to you."

"I'll go get it and we'll turn those weeds under for

you." I returned a few minutes later with the tiller. The ground was fairly hard and hadn't been tilled for several years. We bounced merrily around with the tiller without doing much harm to the ground. "Why don't we put the water on it for a little while and I'll come back this afternoon and turn it under," I suggested.

Patrick nodded, and turned on the sprinklers that covered the garden area. "I really don't want to take all your time," he said.

"No problem. Just leave the water on for an hour or so and I'll come back later." I wheeled the tiller back home.

Later that afternoon I returned to the Jenkinses' backyard. As soon as I started the tiller, Patrick came out the back door. "Can you wait for a minute?" he asked. "Mother would like to see this." I waited until he wheeled his wife around the corner of the house and adjusted her in the shade beneath the chestnut tree. I started the tiller and began turning over the garden area. An hour later I'd made a couple of passes in each direction. The garden looked much better. I started home.

"Wait!" called Patrick over the sound of the motor. "Mother wants to thank you." He motioned me over to his wife's chair. I stopped the tiller and walked over to Virginia. She reached up with her good hand, squeezed mine, and patted me on the arm. Her face beamed a radiant smile. "We don't know how to repay you," said Patrick.

"Happy to do it," I said, and started home with my tiller.

The next morning in church Virginia squeezed my arm and smiled into my face. Patrick thanked me for all of the work in his yard.

The following Saturday I walked over to the Jenkinses' home again. Although it was fairly late in the season to plant a garden, Patrick had planted rows of tomato plants, beans, peppers, cucumbers, and lettuce. "Had to put in container-grown ones this year," he said. "Next year I'm going to start my own. Mother and I are going to build a little greenhouse in the basement workroom." He paused. "Oh, by the way, I noticed your tiller was running a little rough last week. I hope you don't mind, but I tuned it up for you."

"Not at all, I appreciate it," I said. When I got home I looked at my tiller. Every speck of dirt had been wiped from it, the rust spots had been painted over, and it sported a new set of tines. I pulled the starter rope. It started on the first pull and ran better than it had in years.

A few mornings later a crew of ten or twelve men appeared outside the Jenkinses' home. By the time they left that evening the entire outside of the house had been painted. The siding shone bright white. The murky olive trim had been painted forest green.

"Your house looks marvellous," I said to Patrick the next morning.

"Mother's happy with it." He indicated Virginia sitting beneath the chestnut tree. "Our boys did a good job."

"Were all of those men your sons?" I asked.

"Our family," he smiled. Virginia nodded happily.

By the end of the summer the Jenkinses' garden was yielding produce by the bushel. Every plant had been individually tended by Patrick. No weeds grew in his hand-groomed garden. Two or three times a week Patrick waited for the blue Honda to pull up. Then he filled his garden cart with tomatoes and cucumbers and left Virginia to her daughter's care while he walked through the neighborhood distributing vegetables from his cart.

Frost finally came. I turned their garden under with our tiller. As the weather grew colder, Patrick no longer pushed Virginia out beneath the tree each day. When I came home from work I'd look at the picture window in their front room. Often Virginia was sitting there. I'd wave and she'd return my wave.

Thanksgiving morning dawned bright, clear, and cold. Early in the morning the cars began to arrive across the street. By ten o'clock, well over a dozen were parked in their driveway and on the street. The phone rang. It was Patrick. "I don't want to bother you on this Thanksgiving Day, but do you by chance have any folding chairs we could borrow? We thought we'd borrowed enough from the church, but we've come up about six short."

"We've got eight of them," I replied. "I'll bring them over."

"Oh," he said, "the boys and I can come and get them. We don't want to put you out."

I had carried four of the chairs onto the front porch, when two young men approached from across the street. I couldn't help notice how different they looked from each other. One was a tall, skinny blond with piercing blue eyes. The other was short, and dark enough to have been Polynesian. We carried the chairs to the Jenkinses' home. Patrick had not only been working on the outside of the home but been remodeling the inside of the house as well. A wall had been removed and an enormous dining room created. In that room were nearly four dozen people, with Virginia seated at one end of the table in her wheelchair, and Patrick at the other. There were people with red, blond, brunette, and black hair. Their skin tones ran from white to chocolate. Patrick leapt to his feet, his eyes glistening. "Family, our good friend and neighbor." He put his arm around my shoulders. Then, indicating the others, he said, "My family. No. Our family." He beamed at his wife. There were greetings from the group mingled with Patrick's effusive thanks for the chairs.

I turned to go. Patrick said, "Wait just a moment. Mother has been working very hard these past few weeks." The room grew silent. All eyes turned toward Virginia. She smiled. Then a look of enormous concentration appeared on her face. Her lips tensed, and with great effort she said, "Dhang you fo' gummin'." She relaxed and smiled. Patrick beamed while we all applauded.

That evening as Patrick and I carried the chairs back to my home, he said, "That was probably quite a shock to you, meeting our family all at one time."

"Just a little confusing, is more like it."

Patrick sank into the couch in my living room. "Mother and I have never been able to have any children of our own," he began. "So we just helped raise kids that nobody else wanted. Some of them came from racially mixed parentage. Some were crippled or handicapped in some way. Mother just raised them as if they were her own. Not all of them have turned out as well as we'd hoped, but most have. I think nearly everybody responds to love and kindness, don't you?"

I nodded.

"About fifteen years ago Mother had her first stroke," Patrick continued. "I realized we probably couldn't continue taking in any more kids. It just about killed her. But our children—and they really are our children, you know—have been so good. They come by and check on us. We've tried to be as independent as we can, but it's still good to know someone cares. They give Mother a reason to live and to keep trying to recover. She worked so hard to be able to greet our family." His eyes brimmed with tears. "I've got to get home to her. She's a real treasure, my boy."

The following Sunday was the first one in December, which meant we would be having a fast and testimony meeting at church. After the opening hymn and prayer, a baby was blessed. The sacrament was passed, and then it was time for testimony bearing. Patrick Jenkins pushed his wife's wheelchair to the front of the chapel. He picked up the microphone that had been used by the father who had blessed his son. "My dear brothers and sisters," began Patrick, "my wife and I have lived in this ward for over six months, and in that time we've never taken advantage of the opportunity to bear our testimonies." He brushed his white hair back from his forehead. "You have taken us in and made us feel so welcome. My dear wife has trouble speaking, as you know, but she would like to say something to you today." He placed the microphone in front of Virginia's lips.

The room grew quiet as she struggled for a moment and then said, "Read!" She smiled.

Patrick said very quietly, "She would like me to read two of her favorite hymns. They express her testimony. Please follow with us 'I Know That My Redeemer Lives' and 'Count Your Blessings.'" No one made a sound as Patrick Jenkins read the message of these two hymns. Nor was there any question that she believed what he read. She indeed, wheelchair-bound and all, felt herself truly blessed. Patrick wheeled his wife back to his seat.

She died before the winter snows melted. Patrick continued to tend the garden that spring and summer, but the spring was gone from his step. "I never got her greenhouse built," he said humbly. "She did so like to see things grow." He joined her before Thanksgiving.

10

A Broken Heart

Pete Walker was the meanest man I'd ever met. Of course I was only twelve years old, but my mother, who was usually quite charitable, didn't think much of Pete either. He lived in one of the older homes in our community. It was built of rock and was set back behind two oversized pine trees. The lawn that survived the neglect of infrequent watering was rarely mowed. Pete moved into the house about five years before my family moved into the neighborhood. My friends warned me to stay away from Pete's house.

In The Church of Jesus Christ of Latter-day Saints, at the age of twelve most young men have the Aaronic Priesthood conferred on them and are ordained to the office of deacon in that priesthood. One of the duties that deacons have is to collect fast offerings. On the first Sunday of each month Latter-day Saints go without food for two meals and contribute at least the cost of those meals to the poor. Deacons are sent throughout the ward to collect these contributions.

After I was ordained a deacon, my first fast Sunday approached. "Who wants district five?" called out Brother Mangus, the financial clerk of the ward. No one volunteered. "Perhaps we ought to give our new deacon that district." He handed me the ten envelopes with an elastic band around them. There was a collective sigh of relief from the rest of the quorum.

I pulled the elastic band from around the envelopes and looked at the name on the first envelope: "Pete Walker." I understood why no one had volunteered for this district.

Although the sun was shining brightly as I slowly crept up his sidewalk, gloom gathered around me. Timidly I stuck my finger forward to ring his doorbell. There was no answer. I heaved a sigh of relief and turned to leave his porch. Suddenly the door behind me was snatched open!

"Whadda ya want?" Pete bellowed. A wave of stale air laced with sweat assaulted my nostrils. "Oh, it's you, kid." He pushed open the screen door and stuck out his filthy hand. I looked into his bloodshot eyes as I handed him the fast-offering envelope. "Wait here," he commanded as he stepped back into his house and shut the door. My heart pounded as I stood on his porch waiting. At length the door flew open and he handed me the envelope. "Now, get outta here!" He brushed the hair out of his eyes with one hand as he waved me away with the other.

I ran down his sidewalk and onto the street. The rest of my fast-offering district was easy. I returned to the ward house and handed the envelopes to Brother Mangus. "Thank you," he said. "This was your first time, wasn't it?" I nodded my head. "Well, I hope you had a good experience." I rolled my eyes and left the clerk's office.

On the Sunday before Christmas I was passing the sacrament—one of the other duties of deacons—and there on the back row sat Pete Walker. He had made an attempt to comb his hair and beard and was wearing fairly clean clothing. I saw him in church the following Easter Sunday. Over dinner my father said, "Looks like Brother Walker's a regular attender. He regularly attends twice a year." He laughed.

For two years I collected fast offerings from Pete Walker. The routine never varied. And I never saw Pete outside his home except at Christmas and Easter. I wondered what he did for a living. No one seemed to know.

When I was fifteen, Martha Louise Draper moved into our ward. The first Sunday she came to church I fell in love with her. I wasn't alone. I think she captured the hearts of every one of the boys in the Aaronic Priesthood. It mattered not to me that she was ten years older than I; she was the girl of my dreams. I learned later in life that commercial advertisers look for girls like Martha Louise—girls who exude a wholesome beauty—to use in their advertisements. She was blond and pink-cheeked. She smiled freely and displayed even, white teeth. Five minutes after meeting her you felt as if you were old friends. There were only two apartments in our neighborhood. Martha Louise rented the one across the street from Pete Walker.

I found numerous excuses for walking down the street in front of Martha Louise's apartment in hopes that she'd appear. Throughout the summer I continued my excursions. However, I rarely saw her, except at church.

As the summer drew to a close, my friends and I tried to squeeze the last drop of joy from vacation before school began. We rode bicycles ten miles to Lagoon, a local amusement park, and spent our summer wages riding the roller coaster and vainly trying to win prizes on the midway. And then it was over. We glumly boarded the school bus the next morning and rode to school. We grumbled and complained as we checked our schedules for the hundredth time. "Who'd you get for history? Holgren? Forget it!"

The bus ride ended, and I made my way to my first-period class, English. As I walked through the door my perspective on school changed. There stood my teacher, Martha Louise Draper! I thanked whatever fates had arranged my schedule. "Sister Draper," I said, waving at her.

"*Miss* Draper," she replied, smiling. "It's good to see a friendly face. I hope we have a great time this year."

I nodded my head. I now had a reason to come to school. I was certain my attendance would be perfect this year. Class began. Miss Draper led us through the intricacies of Elizabethan sonnets that first term. Never before had I been so captivated by poetry. The end of the term approached.

"I can't believe it!" My mother rolled her eyes as she opened the mail.

My father took the open letter from her hand. It was a wedding invitation. My father's mouth dropped open as he read it. "He's got to be at least fifteen years older than her," he said.

"More like twenty, I'd say," replied my mother.

"Who?" I asked.

"Pete Walker," said my mother. "He's marrying that sweet little Draper girl."

My heart dropped into my shoes. Not my Miss Draper. Not Pete Walker. I picked up the invitation and read it: "Mr. and Mrs. Nolan Draper announce the marriage of their daughter, Martha Louise, to Peter I. Walker, son of the late Mr. and Mrs. Carl Walker. A reception will be held in their honor November 17, from 7:00 until 9:00 P.M., at the home of the bride's parents, 935 East Fountain Avenue. Your presence is the only gift the couple requests."

I thought of how terribly different these two people were. He was so dirty, so unkempt, so uneducated. She was so clean, so pristine, so . . . so . . . so perfect. It was easy to see what he'd seen in her, but what in the world had she seen in him? My heart was crushed.

After dinner I went for a walk. An unseen magnet pulled me toward Martha Louise's apartment. I turned the corner and walked down the street. I looked longingly in her direction. Then, with hate born of jealousy, I looked at Pete Walker's house. The lawn had been cut. The trees had been trimmed. The last remnants of flowers lined the walk. Begrudgingly I thought, *At least he's started taking better care of his house.* I wept as I thought of the two of them living there together.

I went to the wedding reception hoping against hope that the marriage had been called off and Miss Draper was still eligible. She wasn't, but she looked radiant. Pete's hair had been cut, his beard trimmed, and his hands washed. I shook his hand, holding back my jealous anger. Then I grasped Miss Draper's—no, Mrs. Walker's—hand. I tried to summon up courage to kiss the bride, but she thanked me for coming and introduced me to her maid of honor before I could do anything that foolish. I went home, made my way to my bedroom, and wept.

The rest of the school year crept by, and at last vacation began. The first Sunday in June, Mrs. Walker stood in church to bear her testimony. "My dear brothers and sisters, I do so want to thank you for the warm reception I have felt in this ward. Of course it was here I met my dear husband." A gentle murmur drifted through the congregation. I noted with some self-satisfaction that although their house looked much better, Pete still attended church only on Christmas and Easter.

"It has been a hard six years for him. When his mother and father and wife were killed so tragically, he tried to put those memories behind him. That's when he sold his home and moved into this ward. It hasn't been easy for him to work two jobs and go to school. After we married I tried to get him to quit one job. He's too independent. But this next weekend he'll graduate with a master's degree in engineering. He's taken a job with an engineering firm in Arizona, so this will be our last Sunday in this ward. I want to thank you for all of your love and concern for us." She bore her testimony of the truthfulness of the gospel, finished, and sat down. The following week they moved.

My heart healed slowly. The years drifted by. Thirty years passed. My brother-in-law invited us to the baptismal service for my nephew. We travelled the twenty-five miles to their home the following Saturday. We walked into the chapel and sat down. There were six children dressed in white, waiting to be baptized. My brother-in-law and nephew sat on the front row, while the rest of us sat further back in the chapel. I glanced toward a woman sitting across the aisle from me. A vague memory stirred in my mind. The service began. Following an opening hymn and prayer, a short talk was given about baptism. The man who was conducting said, "We're delighted to have six candidates for baptism today. We'd like each of their bishops to come forward and introduce the candidates from their wards. Let's start with the First Ward, Bishop Walker."

A handsome man in his late fifties rose and walked to the stand. He beamed a serene smile as he called my nephew to the stand. After the introduction they walked hand in hand back to the first row, where my nephew sat down next to his father. The bishop continued down the aisle and sat across from me. He smiled at me, and then his brow furrowed. I took a second look at the woman sitting next to him, and realized it was Martha Louise Draper Walker! I looked in amazement at the silver-haired man in the navy blue suit sitting next to her. Bishop Pete Walker!

Following the baptismal service I walked to Bishop Walker and shook his hand. "I used to collect fast offerings from you," I said. A look of recognition swept over his face.

"I'm sorry," he said, "I don't remember your name." His wife stepped to his side and helped.

"Let me introduce you to one of my old students," she said. She completed the introduction. I introduced them both to my wife. "What are you doing now?" Sister Walker asked.

"I'm teaching school," I said. "Computer science and data processing. You inspired me to go into teaching. Obviously you're living here now. The last time I heard you speak, you were going to Arizona."

"You have a good memory. That's been a long time ago. Well, Pete and I lived in Phoenix for nearly five years before we had an opportunity to move back to Utah. We've lived here for nearly twenty-five years. Pete started his own firm about fifteen years ago."

"I'm being really nosy," I said, "but when I used to go collect fast offerings, your husband scared me to death. How in the world did the two of you ever get together?"

She smiled a sweet, serene smile. "One night as I was coming home from school late, I pulled up in front of my apartment and switched off the key in my car. The car kept on running for several seconds. Pete pulled into his driveway about the same time. He came across the street and asked if I needed some help with my car. He was covered with grease and had his bushy beard and hairdo. My first inclination was to run into my apartment and lock the door, but he told me he lived across the street and he'd be happy to adjust my car. I don't know what he did to it, but it ran perfectly.

"I took him a plate of cookies to thank him and we sat on his porch and talked. One thing led to another and we got married."

Bishop Walker said, "This great lady saw right through the dirt, the grease, and the defenses and helped me rebuild my life."

"Would you share your story with us?" I asked.

He nodded his head. "It might take a few minutes. You probably want to visit with your family."

I explained to my brother-in-law that we'd be a few minutes late, and my wife and I made our way to Bishop Walker's office, where we joined the bishop and his wife. We seated ourselves. Bishop Walker rested his chin on his tented hands. "I went on a mission to the Southern States and returned home to a girl who waited for me. We renewed our romance, and about six months later we were married in the Salt Lake Temple. We were driving home to Provo for our reception. I was driving, my new wife was beside me, and my mother and father were in the backseat." His face grew dark as he remembered. "We ran into fog at the Point of the Mountain. I probably wasn't paying as much attention as I should have been. I was probably going too fast. Whatever the case, suddenly I saw brake lights in front of me. I slammed on the brakes and the car skidded sideways into the truck whose brake lights I'd seen."

Tears rolled down his cheeks. "My wife, my father, and my mother were killed. My face slammed into the steering wheel. I broke my jaw, both arms, assorted ribs." He paused for a moment. "I couldn't even attend their funerals; I was in the hospital in traction. We were going to live in my folks' basement apartment. I'm an only child, and when I was finally released from the hospital I returned home to too many memories. The house was mine, but so were the funeral expenses. It took all the money from the sale of the house, plus some more, to pay off all my folks' expenses. My dad didn't believe in life insurance. He thought he was never going to die."

He paused again. "I'm sorry, I'm boring you."

"No, no you're not. Please go on."

"I moved to your ward. I tried to put memories behind me. I thought God had forsaken me. I don't think you can imagine how much guilt I felt. I grew a beard to cover the scars on my face, and I went into seclusion. It didn't take long before I realized I had to go to work, but I really didn't have many skills. I finally got a job at an all-night service station and truck stop. I enrolled at the university and got a part-time job on campus. It took me six years, but I finished my degree. Of course, along the way I ran into Martha Louise."

This time the pause was long enough that I thought Bishop Walker had finished his story. But he cleared his throat and continued: "Do you remember the Lord's statement to Samuel that 'man looketh on the outward appearance, but the Lord looketh on the heart'? Well, Martha Louise went about it the Lord's way. She looked right past the dirty, sweaty, shaggy outward appearance and accepted me as a son of God. There is no doubt in my mind that she saved me from myself." His eyes shone as he looked at his wife. "Gently she brought me back. She loved me into submission. She gave up her great love of teaching her students in order to focus her energy on me. I was frightened to shave my beard. I thought the scars would be too obvious. The scars were more inside than out. It took nearly a year before I started attending church regularly. One day she said, 'Pete, I'm sure the Lord has forgiven you for the accident. Now, when can you forgive yourself?' I realized I'd been blaming God for something I'd done. She is my most treasured companion. She and the Lord together are my salvation." He leaned over and kissed his wife.

My wife and I thanked him and left, hand in hand. "Thank you," I said to her.

"For what?"

"For loving me, with all my imperfections."

She squeezed my hand.

11

The First Mother

Geri and I met, dated for a year, and married. We were no different than many newlyweds. We struggled, disagreed, and laughed a lot during our first year of marriage. The love we believed so strong during our dating year matured, deepened, and turned into real love. A year and a half after our marriage our first child was born, a son, Derick. Over the next dozen years Sharlene, Rebecca, David, Sherri, and Kati were born. Each one different, each occupied a unique niche in our family.

As our children grew older and college expenses and missionary service loomed before us, we decided to open a swimming school. My wife's family had operated one for many years, so we didn't make the decision lightly, nor did we enter the responsibilities it entailed blindly. There were many advantages to the swimming school. Our children learned responsibility as they filled different jobs around the pool. Since I taught school, I had the summer free. Geri and I taught lessons. Derick helped lifeguard. Sharlene ran the office for open plunge, a two-hour free swimming period for anyone who was taking lessons or who lived in the neighborhood. Rebecca made snow cones. David picked up snow cone cups from around the yard.

As the years progressed, so did our children and their responsibilities. When Derick turned seventeen and was eligible to get his water safety instructor's training from the Red Cross, he began teaching. In time Sharlene and Rebecca followed suit. By this time Sherri and Kati were handling the snow cone patrol.

One problem with a swimming school is that it robs you of your opportunity to take vacations. We slipped away to the nearby canyons for overnight camping on the Fourth of July holiday weekend, but we really had no time for an extended family vacation. The solution we reached was to buy a boat and spend as much time as we could together as a family. With Willard Bay and Pineview Reservoir less than an hour away, we often finished open plunge at five o'clock and spent the evening waterskiing and knee boarding. Saturdays we invited family and friends and headed out with the boat.

Time passed, and Derick began attending school at the University of Utah. In due time he approached the bishop, filled out his papers, and received his mission call in August. He was to enter the Missionary Training Center on November 2. Our bishop asked our family to speak in sacrament meeting October 30.

We decided to close the swimming school one session early and take a family boating trip to Lake Powell. It is a bittersweet moment when you realize your children are growing up and going their separate ways. While we rejoice in their growth, we can't help fear for them as they leave the protection of the nest. We want them to go; we just don't want them to leave.

Tents, sleeping bags, clothing, and coolers full of food were secured in the boat. The backseat of our van was removed and foam pads rolled out so that tired children could take a nap on the six-hour ride to Lake Powell. Everyone took a last-minute trip to the bathroom before we headed down the road on our last vacation as a family. We stopped in Provo, Price, and Green River for bathroom breaks. We secretly believed Kati was gathering information for a book on the rest rooms of Utah. At last we reached Bullfrog Basin at Lake Powell. It took two trips in the boat to get the gear and family to Hansen Canyon, where we pitched our tent.

That evening as we ate dinner, Geri complained about not being able to eat much. "I feel stuffed," she said. That night as we sat on the beach watching the houseboat lights in the main channel, she complained again of feeling full. "I feel like I've overeaten, and I haven't had much of anything to eat all day."

The next morning we set off for Rainbow Bridge, several miles down the lake. We were cruising down the main channel at about twenty-five knots, when we were overtaken by a much larger boat. It passed about twenty feet from our port side. Its wake was higher than our boat. I turned into the wake to avoid taking water, and we were slammed fairly hard into the trough. Geri moaned loudly. "That felt like I jammed a rock into my stomach." We continued to Rainbow Bridge, and on the way back to camp I could tell she was hurting.

"Do you want to go home?" I asked as we arrived

back in Hansen Canyon. "We can pack up and head out if you're not feeling well."

"It's just indigestion. I'm going to lie down for a little while. Why don't you take the kids out skiing?" That evening she was feeling no better. "It's just like I have a big rock in my stomach. I feel stuffed. But I'll be OK. We don't want to cut short our vacation. We don't get them very often."

Three days later we left Lake Powell and headed home. Other than feeling bloated, Geri seemed to have little discomfort. However, the next morning she made a doctor's appointment. Our family doctor was one of the last doctors in America to make house calls. He was our trusted neighbor and friend. After he examined Geri, he called the two of us together. "I'd like to have a specialist take a look at you," he said to my wife. "Just better to be safe than sorry." It was obvious he was worried.

Three days later my father-in-law and I sat waiting in my wife's hospital room. "I hate hospitals," he said. "They're full of sick people."

The door opened and there stood one of my dear and valued friends, Ray. "I was sitting at my desk," he said, "and just got this strong impression I needed to come to the hospital and be with you."

I introduced Ray to my father-in-law. We engaged in idle talk for a few moments before the door opened again. The doctor entered. He still had his surgical mask hanging around his neck. "There's no easy way to tell you what I have to say."

My father-in-law sat down heavily on the bed.

Looking at me, the doctor continued: "Your wife's condition is incurable but treatable. We've removed a tumor the size of a football from her abdomen. The omentum, gallbladder, and ovaries were involved. At the moment we think we'll do a fairly heavy chemo-therapy routine. She should have at least two years of good quality life. I wish I had better news. It's never easy. Your wife's in the recovery room. She'll be coming up here as soon as we have her stable." He turned and left.

My mother-in-law had died of cancer five months earlier and my father-in-law was still suffering from that loss. He hugged me, then made an excuse and left to be alone with his thoughts. Ray and I wept. We knelt at the side of her bed and prayed. I remember little of that prayer except that during it a remarkable feeling of peace came over me. We stood up and held each other. "You're going to be all right, aren't you?" said Ray. I nodded my head. "Peace, my friend," he said as he left.

As I waited for my wife to be brought to her room, I thought back over the past twenty-two years. Peculiarly my thoughts went to a list I drew up shortly after our marriage. We wrote down things we'd like to do. Most of them we'd accomplished. Four years before, we'd run the St. George Marathon. Our goal was to run the twenty-six miles in under four hours. I beat four hours by three minutes. Geri beat me by five minutes. Two years before, we'd taken our first jump from an airplane. As she jumped from the plane she let out a whoop that I could hear on the ground five thousand feet below. We still hadn't visited Hawaii. *Maybe we can do that sometime during the next two years,* I thought.

Geri was wheeled into her hospital room and lifted onto the bed. I waited for her to wake up. And wondered how to tell her the news. There is no easy way.

Later that night I went home, gathered our children around me, and told them what the doctor had told me. They agreed that we needed to make the most of the time we had to share.

Ten days later, following chemotherapy, Geri came home. She was still very weak from the surgery and therapy but eager to get on with life. Her doctor made an appointment to see her in two weeks. Our neighbors responded with food and visits and care. Our ward Relief Society president organized the flow of food and the offers of help. I was an assistant principal at one of the local high schools, which gave me some more latitude with my schedule than I'd have had as a teacher. I was able to come home and fix lunch every day and respond to any emergency calls.

Two weeks dragged by until we journeyed to the doctor's office. He checked the progress of her recovery and sent her home. The side effect of chemotherapy appeared one morning as her hair began to fall out. We bundled her up and and drove to a wig shop and solved that problem. The doctor might have been satisfied with her progress, but Geri was not. She continued to lose weight and didn't seem to be regaining any energy or stamina. What bothered her more was that she was still feeling quite a bit of pain.

Late one Saturday night I watched her sleeping fitfully. I knelt down at her bedside and prayed. *Father, I begun, I am so frightened. My dear wife doesn't seem to be getting any better. Day by day I see her slipping a little. Father, I'm selfish, and I'm frightened. I can't raise these six children without her help. I don't want to lose her. We've been through a lot together, and I don't want to lose her. But I don't want to see her suffer, either. Help me, Father. Please help me.*

A feeling of complete calm came over me. Then the Spirit whispered: *She is yours for as long as you desire. But she will never be free from pain. You must decide.*

Oh, I cried inwardly in anguish. *I don't want to lose her. But, more than that, I can't stand to see her in pain.* I continued my prayer, thanking my Father in Heaven for the many, many blessings he had given me.

You have decided well, my son, the Spirit whispered.

The next morning I drove our children to church. After sacrament meeting, while they went to their Sunday School and Primary classes, I went home to see if Geri needed anything. I sat on the edge of our bed and looked at this beautiful partner of mine. Her eyes opened and she said, "I wish I were going to be able to be at Derick's farewell next Sunday." She paused, her eyes opened wider, and she said, "I will be, won't I?" For the first time she admitted that death was near. We wept together. "We need to talk," she said. "We've always set goals together, and we've always tried to get the kids to set goals. I've developed a different perspective in the last few weeks. I want to talk to each of our kids, and then we need to talk."

I picked our children up from church, and one by one their mother talked to them. She talked about the future, about their strengths, about things they needed to guard against. After the children were in bed, Geri and I talked. "I want you to remarry," she said. "You need a wife, and these children need a mother."

"I can't even think about that right now," I said.

"You need to. I've given quite a bit of thought to it and I want you to get married quickly. I've prayed about it and I know who you ought to marry." She named an acquaintance of ours who was single. "You won't understand this," she continued, "but I'm not jealous of her and she won't be jealous of me."

"Well," I said, "I don't think I'm going to worry about that right now. I'm not sure I'm ready to think about marrying someone else."

Geri became very serious. "Listen to me. I want you to marry quickly. By the end of the year. If you don't do it quickly, you'll find excuses why you don't think you should. Just do it!"

I think I can empathize somewhat with those men who entered into plural marriage and whose first wives selected subsequent wives for them. I changed the subject.

The next morning I called Geri's doctor. "Bring her in first thing tomorrow morning," he said. "About nine o'clock."

I started to protest that she needed to go in immediately, but a feeling of peace came over me and I agreed to the Tuesday appointment. When we arrived at his office, the doctor took one look at Geri and re-admitted her to the hospital. I sat in her room while she lay in bed. "Don't forget what I said. You have two months to remarry."

"Can you imagine the gossip that would cause?" I chuckled.

"I'm serious," she replied. "If you love me and if you believe we've had a good marriage, then the best way you can show it is by marrying again. Can you see that?"

I shrugged my shoulders. "I'm not sure the neighbors would understand your logic."

She smiled. "When have you ever worried about what others think? Just do what is right. Get married—if you love me."

She was wheeled off to surgery, while I waited in her room. An hour later her doctor entered. "The tumor has grown back," he said hopelessly. "I think we ought to let her go." I nodded in agreement. "She'll probably not regain consciousness. We've got her pretty doped up for the pain." He appeared very,

very tired. "I don't know how long it will be. Her heart's strong—probably a week or so." He took my hand. "I wish I had better news."

"Doctor, I want to tell you three things. First, we know you did your best. Second, she will wake up because she wants to say good-bye to her children. And third, she won't last more than a day or two."

He shook his head and smiled weakly. "I'm sorry, so sorry." He left the room.

I went home and gathered our children around me. We wept together. "Dad," said Rebecca, "you've taught us about life after death. Are you sure, really sure, about that?"

"Oh yes. More certain than I ever thought possible."

"Then," she said, "we'll see Mom again, won't we?"

A deep peaceful feeling filled the room.

The next afternoon I sat at Geri's bedside stroking her hand and keeping quiet watch over her sleeping figure, when the door opened. There stood the sister whom Geri had told me to marry. "I'm not sure why I'm here," she said. "I hate hospitals. I wouldn't even visit my grandfather when he was ill. But I'm here. Why don't you go home and take care of your kids. I'll stay here with Geri." I thanked her and left.

I went home, fixed dinner, fed the kids, and had family prayer with them before we all returned to the hospital. As we entered Geri's room, our friend jumped to her feet. "I've got to go," she blurted, and started toward the door.

"What's the matter? You look like you've seen a ghost." I exclaimed.

"I can't talk about it now. Maybe later."

"What happened? Did Geri wake up?"

She paused at the door. "No. She's still asleep. But we've been communicating . . . I really can't explain it, but . . ." She left the sentence hanging. "We've got to talk, but not right now." She fled down the hall.

Our six children gathered around their mother. Her eyelids fluttered and she opened her eyes. A smile formed on her lips. There were gentle hugs and tears and farewells. "I'm ready to go," she said. "There's no one in this world I have ill feelings toward. I've tried to do my best. I love you. Would you please give me a blessing and release me?" Derick, our soon-to-be-missionary, and I complied.

She slipped back into unconsciousness. I took the children home. A few hours after I returned to the hospital, Geri died.

The next three days passed quickly. Sunday's sacrament meeting was Derick's missionary farewell. I delivered my message of love and encouragement to him and then told him what his mother asked me to say for her. That evening we held a viewing at the local funeral home.

Monday, Halloween day, was Geri's funeral. For twenty-two years we kissed each other good-bye as I left for work, and said, "Have a good day. I'll see you later." As we prepared to close the coffin I bent over and kissed my wife good-bye. "Have a good eternity," I said. "I'll see you later."

"And the peace of God, which passeth all understanding," as the Apostle Paul wrote, came upon my family.

12

The Second Mother

Following Geri's death our family struggled as we redefined our individual roles. The lady whom Geri had chosen for my second wife was reluctant to assume that position. I foolishly tried to pretend that nothing had changed and that a replacement wife would fill the niche left by the departing one. At first the woman and I made an attempt to honor Geri's wishes. We dated a few times and acted as if things would work out, but they didn't.

Friends began to approach me. Uncertain how to begin, most would say, "Would you do me a favor? There is this woman I know who is such a good person. Would you mind calling her and taking her out to dinner?" And I would.

In all fairness, they were all lovely women. Some had never married, and some had lost their husbands to death or divorce; but all were lovely women. The evenings were pleasant ones.

The secretary at the school where I was assistant principal said one day, "I have a friend who is just a neat lady. Would you call her and take her to dinner?"

"I'll be happy to, but I'm really tied up with registration right now. Let me get it out of the way and then I'd be happy to take your friend to dinner. What's her name?"

"Janice. We used to live across the street from each other. You'll like her."

"I'm sure I will. Just let me get registration over, OK?"

My secretary nodded. A few days later a note appeared on my desk calendar—"Call Janice for dinner," followed by a phone number. I smiled and continued to work on registration. Several more notes appeared on following days. At length I completed registration.

"Have you called Janice yet?" asked my secretary one Thursday afternoon. "I know she isn't busy tomorrow night. You promised you'd call her, remember?"

"I remember." I picked up the phone and dialed. A teenaged boy answered.

"Mom," he yelled, "it's for you."

We went to dinner the following evening. Janice found out about my six children and I found out about her two boys. Just as my oldest, Derick, was on a mission for The Church of Jesus Christ of Latter-day Saints in California, her oldest son, Stan, was on a mission in Ireland. Her younger son, Brett, was fifteen; my Rebecca was sixteen, and David was fourteen. We talked about the singles program in the Church. Janice was in charge of singles events for her stake. "Have you ever been to a singles dance?" she asked.

I had avoided singles dances. "No," I said. "Most of my Friday nights are tied up with school events. I'm surprised I didn't have anything going on tonight."

"There's a dance tomorrow night," said Janice. "You ought to drop in just to see what they're like. We're in charge of refreshments." I assumed a noncommittal expression.

We pulled into her driveway after dinner. A roving band of neighborhood teens saw us pull in and wandered over. "Hi, Mom," called out one of the girls. Janice had been her teacher in the Young Women organization at church. Suddenly she said brightly, "Hi, Mr. Siddoway." I recognized her as one of the girls I had taught to swim. We were surrounded by a swarm of chaperones.

The following day I completed some chores around the house and sat down in front of the TV set. Sharlene, my eighteen-year-old said, "Did you have a good time last night, Dad?"

"Janice is a lovely lady. We had a pleasant dinner."

"Dad," said Sharlene, "you say 'pleasant' too much. Did you have a good time?"

I thought about it. It had been a very relaxed evening for me, although I sensed Janice was quite nervous. "Yes, yes, I did, Sharlene."

"Are you going to see her again?"

I didn't know whether Sharlene was trying to tell me anything, or whether she was just making "pleasant" conversation, but suddenly I said, "I think I'm going to go down to a singles dance. Janice is helping with the refreshments." A feeling of peace flooded over me.

Half an hour later, showered, shaved, and dressed appropriately, I arrived at my first singles dance. I entered the cultural hall of the church. Within forty-five seconds a lady wearing a black satin dress, a bouffant blond wig, and tap shoes approached me. "You're new here, aren't you?" she queried.

"Yes," I smiled. I have never considered myself the "leading man" type, but as if I were a pot of honey, the bees began to swarm in my direction. I excused myself and headed for the kitchen. Janice was dispensing ice-cream sandwiches. I slipped into the kitchen and offered to help.

The parade of dancers wandered by to pick up the refreshments. "That's Billy White Shoes," whispered Janice, indicating a man with no hair and a bright yellow sport coat. "He's at least ninety, and he finds a singles dance every night of the week. He likes to pinch you while you're dancing with him." I smiled at Billy and handed him an ice-cream sandwich.

"Hey," squawked a woman with flaming red hair and an emerald green gown. "Are you keeping him to yourself, or can anyone get a dance?" She laughed a raucous laugh. I smiled and handed her an ice-cream sandwich. Janice blushed.

When the dance ended we put chairs away together. "How did you like it?" she asked.

"There are some really interesting people here," I answered. "Really interesting."

"They're lonely," said Janice. "I guess these dances fill a need, but sometimes I'm not sure they're what we really need." She shrugged her shoulders. I walked her to her car and drove home in mine.

The following Saturday we went boating. Brett, Rebecca, and David behaved as if they'd known each other all of their lives. In the late afternoon we stowed away the water skis and knee boards and headed home. "Dad," said Rebecca as Janice and Brett pulled out of our driveway, "Brett's cool."

Our society has perpetuated a number of lies. One of the most interesting is the concept that there is only one person you can love. Our literature is full of maidens waiting for their knights on white steeds to sweep them off their feet. The concept seems to be built on the belief that there is some fixed quantity of love built into each of us and it can be bestowed only on a single person. But, as anyone who has more than one child knows, love multiplies with the birth of each child, and we do not have to divide love among our children. But the lie persists.

David approached me, brow furrowed, "Dad, do you still love Mom?"

"Of course. Why do you ask?"

"Well, you and Janice . . ." He shrugged his shoulders. "I mean, are you two getting serious?"

"Not too serious, yet. Does that bother you?"

"I don't know. I mean, I guess I'm just confused."

"David, your mother told me that the best monument I could build to her would be to marry someone. She said that if we'd had a poor marriage, then I probably wouldn't want to marry again, but if we'd had a good marriage, then I ought to get married. Does that make any sense to you?"

"Sort of." His fourteen-year-old mind grappled with this thought.

"David, does it seem to you that I'm being unfaithful to your mother because I've been dating Janice?"

"I don't know. Thanks, Dad." I thought the conversation was over. He turned to leave, then said, "Dad, do you love Janice?"

"I guess I need to find out the answer to that, don't I?"

He shrugged his shoulders.

The next night Janice asked me, "Where is this thing going? If we're going to continue to see each other, we need to answer that question."

"Where do you want it to go?" I asked.

"That's unfair," she said. "I need to know your feelings first."

We sat quietly for a few minutes until I finally said, "You're a very attractive lady, and I feel very much at peace when we're together. I'm not promising anything, but I'd like to keep seeing you, if you feel the same way." She nodded. When I left that night I kissed her good night.

Two weeks later at an outing at Yuba Lake we sat in our boat looking at the stars and I asked her to marry me. Her answer was, "Well, when can you work it into your schedule?"

Three weeks later I married this beautiful woman in the Salt Lake Temple.

One of the other lies our society promotes is that there will be terrible fights when two families are blended together. Immediately after our marriage the entire family became involved in a production of *The King and I*. Janice and I took two weeks out of rehearsal to fly to Ireland and pick up Stan from his mission.

We have supported each other as Stan married Brenda, Derick married Bonnie, and Sharlene married John. When Brett left on a mission for The Church of Jesus Christ of Latter-day Saints, David was perhaps most deeply affected by the temporary loss of his brother.

I have found in Janice a woman who will give anything she owns to anyone in need. She is much better than I in finding those around us who are in need.

One day Kati, who turned eight the year Janice and I married, said to me, "Dad, would it bother you if I called Janice 'Mom'?"

"I'd be overjoyed, Kati."

And so the second mother of our children has

brought her special brand of love to our home. She has mothered my children as her own and allowed me the privilege of adding two great sons to our family. And I can now answer David's question. "Yes, I love her. I love her with a love that grows with each passing day."

One day, recently, a new member of our neighborhood asked, "Now, which of those children are yours and which are Janice's?"

I answered, "I forget. Just like everything else in our lives, they're ours."

About the Author

Richard M. Siddoway was raised in Salt Lake City and Bountiful, Utah. He was educated in Salt Lake City and Davis County schools. He earned both a bachelor's and a master's degree from the University of Utah. A professional educator for over thirty years in Utah and Arizona, he is currently the supervisor of library media services for Davis County School District. He is a former bishop and now serves as a member of the stake presidency in the Val Verda Stake in Bountiful, Utah. He is also the author of the book *Twelve Tales of Christmas*. He and his wife, Janice, have eight children.